Wise Daniel

Our Missionary Heroes and Heroines

Heroic Deeds Done in Methodist Missionary Fields

Wise Daniel

Our Missionary Heroes and Heroines
Heroic Deeds Done in Methodist Missionary Fields

ISBN/EAN: 9783337194352

Printed in Europe, USA, Canada, Australia, Japan

Cover: Foto ©Lupo / pixelio.de

More available books at **www.hansebooks.com**

Our Missionary Heroes and Heroines;

HEROIC DEEDS DONE IN METHODIST MISSIONARY FIELDS.

BY

DANIEL WISE, D.D.,

AUTHOR OF "HEROIC METHODISTS," "SKETCHES AND ANECDOTES OF AMERICAN METHODISTS," ETC.

From old chronicles where sleep in dust
  Names that once filled the world with trumpet tones
  *   *   *   *   *   fashion as I must.
  Quickened are they that touch the prophet's bones.
                                 Longfellow.

NEW YORK:
PHILLIPS & HUNT.
CINCINNATI:
WALDEN & STOWE.
1884.

Copyright 1884, by
PHILLIPS & HUNT,
New York.

PREFATORY NOTE.

THE object of this volume is to deepen the interest of the youth of Methodism in our great missionary work. Its method is not that of the historian or biographer, but of an etcher, seizing on striking facts in the personal history of distinguished missionaries, and portraying them in such lights and shades as may impress the imagination and win the youthful heart to sympathy with the divine work of teaching all nations the words of the Son of God. Hence the heroic side of the missionary character is largely brought into view. Its noble self-consecration upon the altar of Christian charity; its meek spirit of self-denial; its lofty defiance of the perils of the sea, the forest jungle, the deadly fever, and the untutored savage; its sublime patience amid the most appalling difficulties, and its perseverance unto those initial victories which are the sure auguries of the final conquest of the world, are herein outlined in strict harmony with the truth of history.

The writer is aware that less heroism is required in the missionary of to-day than in those who fought and fell in the beginning of the modern missionary crusade. The ægis of the civilized world protects him almost everywhere, and in many nations the work of his predecessors has made it safe for him to preach where they had to do it standing in the jaws of death. Nevertheless, it is not entirely true that the heroic age in missionary history is past. The dangers, self-denials, and sacrifices are less formidable, but they are still of a number and character to forbid any but men and women of a heroic faith in Christ to face them. To exchange life in a Christian land, like ours, for one to be spent in exhausting climates, amid the corruptions of heathen and papal communities, for no other end than to instruct and save them, though less impressive than the trials herein recorded, is itself an act of exalted heroism, and those who are doing it deserve to be ranked among the noblest workers in the Church of the living God.

These etchings are chiefly of the missionary heroes and heroines of our English and American Methodism. And this, not because other Churches have produced no such characters; for, in fact, their missionary records are as rich in noble deeds as our own; but because it is proper that Methodist youth should first be made familiar with the heroic souls of their own Church. Of some of the pioneers of sister Churches who were in the modern foreign missionary field before us, the first chapter treats. Let us honor their memories as we do those of our own Church. And let us read and think of what our own brethren have done and suffered for the cause in missionary fields until our hearts reciprocate their zeal and move us to sustain our missions with gifts sufficient to keep them growing until, like the stone cut out of the mountain without hands, they cover the whole earth.

DANIEL WISE.

ENGLEWOOD, N. J., 1884.

CONTENTS.

CHAPTER I.

SOME MISSIONARY SOCIETY PIONEERS.

The Pilgrim Fathers—Other noble souls—Wesley's Missionary Society—William Carey, the shoe-maker—His heroic offer—Opposition—Wins the Baptists to missionary work—Call to Bengal—His reluctant wife—His success—A consecrated boy—Three Sophomores under a hay-stack—A missionary band—Birthday of the American Board—Five American Missionaries sent to India—American Baptists and Burmah—What a magazine article brought to pass—London Missionary Society—The work of nearly a hundred years................Page 13

CHAPTER II.

LIVES GIVEN TO THE LIBERIAN MISSION.

Who are true heroes—A young invalid at a Conference—His desire—A bishop's question—Melville B. Cox—A grave in Africa anticipated—A grand response—On board the Jupiter—In Monrovia—From Monrovia to heaven—Five more volunteer missionaries—Fever victims—Returning missionaries—A noble-souled lady—Heroism of John Seys and wife—His first night in the death chamber of Cox—His work in Liberia—Ann Wilkins's work—Blissful death........................... 31

CHAPTER III.
A PLOWMAN'S HEROIC ZEAL.

Elisha at the plow—George Piercy hears the call of God—Consulting a friend—Good advice—Waiting—The call repeated—The courage of faith—A depressing voyage—Alone in China—Disheartening information—A Christian soldier—Finding a friend—Doing one's best—Help from home—Among the heathens—Force of example—Accepted by his Church as a missionary—The father of the Wesleyan Missions in China..Page 32

CHAPTER IV.
ON THE BANKS OF THE GAMBIA RIVER.

A tale of death—Its effect on some missionary candidates—William Moister and his bride—On the Gambia—A delightful reception—A good omen—Fruit—A sail up the Gambia—Tornado—The cry for rum—Mrs. Moister's visitors—Sick with fever—War near the mission—On M'Carthy's Island—At King Bruma's palace—Return to England.................... 68

CHAPTER V.
INDIAN VOICES.

Effect of a few words—Seeking for God's Book—A long journey—Its story printed—The call from Wilbur Fisk—Cheerful responses—The land aflame with zeal—In search of the Flatheads—March of our missionaries to Oregon—Teaching the Indians—Preaching to white pioneers—Jason Lee's return for re-enforcements—Great results of the mission......... 84

CHAPTER VI.
HEROIC WORK AMONG NEW ZEALAND SAVAGES.

Waiting for a mission field—A call to New Zealand—The missionary's bride—Arrival at Wangaroa—Building a mission house—The chief, George—A daring deed—Encouragements—The robber chief—The courage of faith—Progress—Narrow escape from death—A captured whale-ship—Persecutions—Flight and return—Tribal wars—Driven from the mission—Fleeing from death—A wife's heroism—Resting at Sydney—Among the Tonguese savages—Sublime madnesss—Success in Tonga—In New Zealand again—Wise counsels—Impaired health—Triumphant death—New Zealand a Christian country...Page 99

CHAPTER VII.
A SHORT BUT BEAUTIFUL LIFE.

A flood of feeling—The young man eloquent—A noble sister—Mr. Bumby in New Zealand—A touching prayer—A terrible chief's conversion—A chief's shrewd reply—Hardships—A notorious man-eater—Making peace between angry cannibal tribes—Wonderful success—A dying missionary's last words—Mr. Bumby's tragic death—His mantle falls on his noble sister—A missionary's dying exclamation 117

CHAPTER VIII.
CONQUEST OF BEAUTIFUL TONGA.

Friendly Islands—Bad qualities of their people—Four missionaries killed or driven off—A missionary's widow—Walter Lawry's sunny reception—Driven away—New missionaries in Tonga—Robbed and threatened—Discouragements—Re-enforcements—A beam of light—Unexpected perils—A friend—A bold reply—A chief's conversion—Showers of blessing—Hanging idols—Eight thousand converts—Christian Tonga........ 133

CHAPTER IX.
A LOVELY AND HEROIC LADY.

A bridal party—A severe struggle—Arrival at Tonga—Kind greetings—Glorious things—A call to Fiji—A horrible feast—

Mrs. Cargill's meek reply—Affectionate farewells—A warlike reception—The cannibal king—An unexpected welcome—First night in Fiji—First converts—A hurricane—Priestly opposition—A shrewd reply—Rich harvests of souls—Mrs. Cargill's beautiful death ....Page 147

CHAPTER X.

GOING TO "CEYLON'S ISLE."

Dr. Coke's grand confession—An undying spark—A noble pledge—Last night in England—At sea—Sickness and death on shipboard—Doctor Coke found dead in his cabin—A stunning blow—Embarrassed missionaries in Bombay—A generous sailor—Friends appear—From Bombay to Ceylon—Cordial welcomes—A ripe field—A Buddhist priest's conversion—The convert's dream—Death of Mr. Ault—The *Ava priest* becomes a Christian—Rich fruits in Ceylon............................ 161

CHAPTER XI.

THE GRAVE-YARD OF MISSIONARIES.

Freed men in Sierra Leone—Their cry for a missionary—The noble volunteer—Reception by the people—Success—Striken to death—Another call—Other responses—Success of Mr. and Mrs. Davies—Mrs. Davies dies—A cry of joy—Burning Greegrees—Calling for help—Fresh reapers sent out—Another missionary's wife dies—Success in winning souls—Driven away by fever—Two more heroes—Still another missionary dies—More sickness—New helpers—Off to the Gambia—Hardships—First convert—Fifty-four missionary volunteers die in forty years—Roland Peck's grand self-devotion—The grave-yard of missionaries 175

CHAPTER XII.
IN THE LAND OF THE NAMAQUAS.

Barnabas Shaw's desire—Sails for the Cape of Good Hope—A discourteous governor—Preaching to soldiers—A missionary visitor—Starting for Namaqua land—A queer traveling machine—Over rough roads—A chief seeking a teacher—Lily Fountain Mission—Teaching and preaching—Privations—First-fruits—Converts—Helpers from England—Escape from a venomous puff-adder—A missionary murdered—Home to rest—Return to Africa—Peaceful death.................Page 189

CHAPTER XIII.
PERILS AND TRIALS OF MISSIONARY LIFE.

Ship on fire—Drifting in an open boat—Friendly missionaries—Books and clothing lost—Another hard voyage—Studying the language—An Indian congregation—Travel in a palankeen—Fording a river—Escape from a serpent—Horrible sights—Scenes of misery—Joy at success—The puff-adder at a missionary's feet—A missionary's ride................... 203

CHAPTER XIV.
TWO MISSIONARY PIONEERS.

A call for a missionary to India—Dr. Butler's response—A sore trial—Selecting a field—Discouraging counsel—Finding a native helper—Beginning work—A war cloud—A perilous flight—In a jungle—Revolt of the bearers—Answer to prayer—A place of refuge—Joel's flight—Another perilous journey—Return to Bareilly—Helpers from America—The mission founded—Its great success—The Pioneer of the South Indian Conference—What led William Taylor to India—His work in Bombay—Organizing a self-supporting Church—Great results—Dr. Taylor's monument. Dr. Taylor made bishop for Africa.......... 221

CHAPTER XV.

SOME HEROIC LADY MISSIONARIES.

Heathen women in India and China—Society of Methodist ladies in America—Their first funds—Their first missionary—Miss Thoburn's success—Their first medical missionary—Miss Fannie J. Sparkes in Bareilly—Nellie—Her consecration to mission work—Her early death—A motherless infant girl dedicated to mission work—Carrie L. M'Millan fulfills her father's vow—Her work for India's daughters—Miss Susan B. Higgins in Japan ....Page 236

CHAPTER XVI.

MISSIONARY SCENES AND INCIDENTS.

A scene in Modena, Italy—A scene in Rome—The fall of Montezuma—Romanism in Mexico—Methodism in Mexico—Romanism a persecutor—A scene in Danville, Ohio—William Nast and German Methodism. Incidents of mission work in India.. 254

Illustrations.

NYNEE TAL..Frontispiece	
MONROVIA	30
OREGON INSTITUTE.....................................	97
SAINT PAUL'S METHODIST EPISCOPAL CHURCH, ROME.....	255
THE HINDUS AND THEIR TEACHER.......................	275

OUR MISSIONARY HEROES AND HEROINES.

CHAPTER I.

SOME MISSIONARY SOCIETY PIONEERS.

> ". . . . He alone, who hath
> The Bible need not stray,
> Yet he who hath, and will not give
> That heavenly guide to all that live,
> Himself shall lose the way."—MONTGOMERY.

WHERE is the boy, where the girl, who does not love to read and re-read the story of those gallant men and brave women who crossed the rough Atlantic Ocean in that frail little vessel named the "Mayflower?" Where is the young heart that has not swelled with admiration when thinking of those noble Pilgrim Fathers and mothers who forsook their homes in England and Holland and came to this then wild land, peopled with savages, not for the sake of gain, but that they might find that freedom to worship God which they were denied in the land of their birth? Those Pilgrim Fathers were, indeed, worthy of your admiration, and they will forever rank in history among the noblest of human kind.

In these sketches of "Missionary Heroes and Heroines" I propose to tell you of other men and women as heroic and noble as our Pilgrim Fathers; of souls whose adventures were as thrilling as theirs, and whose motives were still loftier. For grand as was the object sought by the Pilgrims, it was not wholly unmixed with the hope of gaining lands and building homes that might more than replace those they had forsaken. But our early missionary heroes could indulge no such expectation. As they embarked on the vessels which bore them to the shores of savage and pagan nations, and looked forward to the field of their labors, they could truthfully say, as Wesley did in 1737, that "the difficulties we must encounter God only knows; probably martyrdom will conclude them." Nevertheless, their hearts did not feel the chill of cowardice, neither did their cheeks turn pale. On the contrary, their eyes brightened, their hearts swelled with holy love, and they thought, if they did not say, as did an American missionary, "We would rather be missionaries in yonder dark lands, pointing ignorant heathens to Christ, than to enjoy the pleasures of a civilized and Christian country."

Before telling you of some of these brave souls, whose missionary toils reflect honor on our race and also on our beloved Methodism, I will give you one or two illustrations of the way in which the modern missionary work began in other denominations. As to our Wesley, he took up a missionary collection, at Newcastle, as early as 1767, about the time that the rigging-loft was opened for Methodist preaching in New York city; in 1778 he talked of sending missionaries to Africa, and in 1784 he organized a Methodist Missionary Society. But his preachers were so overloaded with home work and with calls from America that it was scarcely possible to spare men for heathen fields. Nevertheless, the great Wesleyan revival so roused the spiritual slumber of other Churches, that about the close of the century they began foreign missionary work. I will now tell you how the English Baptists were led to start their missions.

About one hundred years ago a young man, named WILLIAM CAREY, was admitted to membership in a Baptist Church in England. This young man was a poor shoe-maker, born of obscure parents, reared in poverty, with very little opportunity to go to school. Perhaps no one, seeing him pulling wax-ends on a cobbler's bench, ever imagined that beneath his coarse vest a great heroic heart was beating. Yet it was even so, for while his hands were busy pounding leather on a lap-stone his active mind was thinking of the facts he learned in his few leisure hours. He thirsted for knowledge. He read history, he studied geography, he learned to draw maps, he acquired several languages, and, after a time, was able, by this self-teaching, to ascend from the cobbler's bench to the desk of a school-teacher. When twenty-two years old he sat at the feet of the Great Teacher, and learned that wisdom which is higher than all the lore of human books. With his wisdom the Saviour gave him the richer pearl of love, and than he began to think of the people who lived in the lands of which he had read so much. These thoughts burned themselves deep into his soul, and soon after, in a monthly prayer-meeting, just then established at Nottingham to pray for the extension of Christ's kingdom, he began telling the people that missionaries might and ought to be sent to heathen nations; and then he would bravely add, "I myself am willing to go."

It seems strange, but it is true, that this heroic offer, instead of kindling missionary fire in the hearts of his Baptist brethren, offended them. The modern missionary spirit had not then quickened the Churches, and, therefore, his burning words, often repeated, led some to say,

"Carey is infatuated!" Others remarked, "Carey's schemes are wild!" Still others said, "Such a project is hopeless;" but here and there was one who pondered on his words, as did Mary of old on the things that related to her divine Child.

One day in a meeting of ministers Mr. Carey wished them to discuss a resolution, that it is "the duty of Christians to attempt the spread of the Gospel among heathen nations," when, strange to tell, he was reproached by a venerable member as an enthusiast for entertaining such a notion.

Heroic souls are undaunted, and Carey, being a genuine moral hero, would not be put down. He wrote on the question, talked about it, and brooded over it until his desire to promote missionary work grew into a mighty masterpassion. At last his missionary zeal begot a kindred fire in some other souls; and eight years from the time of his first public utterance, while preaching a powerful sermon, he conquered the prejudice of his brethren, and they resolved to form a missionary society. As if to prove his own sincerity, he at once offered to go to the South Sea Islands if the means were provided to support him one year. The people in those islands were savages at that time. Yet he stood ready to take his life in his hand that he might tell them the sweet story of his Lord's love. O noble, Christ-like man!

But an opening occurred just then for a mission to Bengal, India. "Will you go to Bengal?" asked his brethren. "I will," he replied most cordially. As a discussion about sending him to this latter place was going on, a gentleman named Thomas, who had been in Bengal, came into the room. Carey rose to greet him, and both were so overcome with feeling that they fell on each other's necks and wept! After hearing Mr. Thomas speak, a Mr. Fuller said:

"From Mr. Thomas's account there is a gold mine in India, but it seems almost as deep as the center of the earth. Who will venture to explore it?"

Then the devoted Carey replied, "I will go down, but remember that you must hold the ropes."

"We will, we will!" responded his brethren with enthusiastic solemnity. Carey's perseverance had won the battle, and henceforth the English Baptist Missionary Society became a power in the heathen world.

Good women are generally willing to work for Jesus anywhere, but Mr. Carey's wife was not willing to go with him to India. Indeed, she declared she would not go. This was a critical test of Carey's loyalty to Christ. But, much as he loved his wife, he loved Christ more, and therefore resolved to go to Bengal without her. Again and again he besought her to change her purpose, apparently in vain. Finally, after bidding her adieu, and then missing the vessel in which he was to sail, he resumed his plea, and, like a true wife, she relented, and sailed with him to his chosen field.

Dr. Carey's personal labors, after many sufferings, achieved much among the pagans, but when he receives his heavenly crown it will surely be adorned with many stars because of the glorious spiritual victories won by that Baptist Missionary Society which his entreaties, undying zeal, and prayers called into being.

Let us now look at the young American who had Carey's spirit, and was the means of starting the American Board of Missions on its grand career.

Boys and girls are often said to be like vessels which have large ears, because they are apt to listen to what grown people say when they are talking about their private affairs. Sometimes they make an ill-use of what they hear. Generally they soon forget what they hear. Now and then words remain in their memories, sink into their deepest thoughts, and give direction to their lives. I will give you an example of this last-named effect of a few words spoken by a mother in the presence of her little son.

This lady, whose name was Mills, was speaking of her son Samuel to a friend one day, when she said, probably with deep and solemn feeling, "I have consecrated this child to the service of God *as a missionary.*"

Little Samuel heard these words. It is doubtful if he understood just what they meant, since missionaries were not much talked about in those days. But he knew they meant something about his own future life, and that led him to think of them and hide them in his memory.

While he was yet a young man he very wisely enlisted under the banner of Jesus. No sooner had he opened his heart to receive a drop of the Saviour's love than those words of his mother grew into a great and grand desire. Then his heart cried, "O that I may become a missionary to the heathen in foreign lands!"

Good desires, like choice plants, need to be kept moist by dew-drops and showers from heaven. Samuel knew this, and all the time he was preparing for college he kept his desire alive by praying for that grace which is a living fountain in the soul. When he entered Williams College, in 1806, he did not suffer thoughtless freshmen to kill his noble desire. One day, about the time of his entrance into the sophomore class, he said to two of his classmates, "Let us take a walk."

Then he led them into a quiet spot, apart from the haunts of college roysterers, and there, while they sat in the shadow of a hay-stack, he told his companions about his heroic desire. It was a pleasant surprise to him to be told that they, too, were cherishing the same sublime wish. They were a happy trio on that memorable day, a portion of which they spent in prayer and in conversation about their chosen plan of life.

This trio, like true knights of the cross, drew other young men into a missionary band resolved to consecrate their lives, not to the pursuit of honor or places of ease or riches, but to preaching the Gospel of love and life to miserable heathen souls—a work that is the noblest of all the works of men. From college these young men went to the Andover Theological Seminary. Others soon caught the heavenly flame, among whom were two, named Judson and Newell.

The resolution of these noble young men to become missionaries was made known, after a time, to the faculty of the institution. These gentlemen approved, and consulted with some distinguished clergymen, two of whom, while riding in a carriage, proposed to form a missionary society. A day or two afterward four of the consecrated band sent a paper to the Congregational Association, on which were these grand words, worthy to be written in letters of gold:

"Our minds have long been impressed with the duty and importance of personally attempting a mission to the heathen."

The next day the Congregational Association instituted that remarkably successful missionary society, popularly known as The American Board, or, as it is more properly called, The Board of Commissioners for Foreign Missions. Some eighteen months later this Board sent out five missionaries to the East Indies. Their names were Judson, Nott, Hall, Newell, and Rice—men worthy of honorable remembrance. And thus you see that a few words, dropped from a loving mother's lips and nourished in the heart of a thoughtful boy, grew into a powerful organization, which has planted its missions in many lands, and led tens of thousands of guilty, miserable souls into the possession of that peace, joy, hope, and eternal life which are the rich fruitage of faith in the Lamb of God who taketh away the sins of the world.

There are rivers which, after flowing short distances from their mountain springs, meet with obstructions that cause their waters to divide into separate streams. And so it happened in the case of this pioneer missionary society. Among its first five missionaries were two, Messrs. Judson and Rice, who, while on their voyage out, thought they saw reasons for adopting the peculiar views of the Baptists. This unlooked-for incident looked at first like a misfortune, but the God of missions so overruled it that it turned out for the furtherance of this infant cause. For after these two young men reached India they wrote to their Baptist friends in America, telling them of their changed opinions on the question of baptism. As their story spread among Baptist churches, the spirit of missions was awakened among them, and they speedily organized a Baptist Missionary Society. Supported by this body, Messrs. Judson and Rice founded missions in Burmah. The work in that country was bitterly, cruelly opposed by the Burmese. But the heroic courage of Judson and his fellow-workers conquered at last, and a most wonderful work was wrought there, especially among the simple-minded Karens, a people subject to the king of Burmah. From that time onward the American Baptists entered heartily into missionary work, sending hundreds of missionaries into the field, and changing thousands of unhappy pagans into happy disciples of the Lord Jesus. And their work must, in part at least, be credited to those few seed-words dropped by Mrs. Mills into the heart of her consecrated boy.

Not far from the time when Carey breathed missionary fire into the souls of his brethren some one wrote an article on missions for the

"London Evangelical Magazine." That article fell like a living spark on many leading men of the English Dissenting Churches, and led to the formation of the London Missionary Society, which soon took a foremost position in the van of the Christian missionary army which God was calling to rise and take possession of the heathen as the promised inheritance of his ever-living Son. Other Churches, both in England and America, soon joined this modern crusade for the spiritual conquest of the nations. Not a hundred years have yet passed since this holy war began in good earnest, yet to-day there are in the great missionary field, as nearly as can be ascertained, not less than five thousand missionaries, more than twenty-five thousand native preachers, and more than fifteen hundred lady missionaries! What has this army of the Lord accomplished? God alone can fully answer this question. But human records show that tens of thousands of heathen souls have no doubt been saved and gone to heaven; probably not less than half a million are now living and serving the Christ, and a million more are being taught the way of life. Of heathen children also there are nearly half a million under Sunday-school instruction. Are not these glorious, abundant, wonderful results in so short a time, and from such feeble beginnings? Behold, O ye youth of Methodism, what God hath wrought!

Monrovia.

CHAPTER II.

LIVES GIVEN TO THE LIBERIAN MISSION.

"He, from duty never altering
Who, with faith's heroic ken,
Forward treads with step unfaltering,
Is the man of men."—D. M. MOIR.

MOST young people love to read about heroic men and women. The soldier who seeks "the bubble reputation at the cannon's mouth," the sailor who prefers sinking with his battered ship to hauling down his country's flag, and the traveler who braves the icebergs of the north or the burning heat of tropical deserts that he may add somewhat to men's knowledge of this great round world, charm their imaginations, and make their hearts swell with admiration. This feeling is proper, and, if fitly guarded, healthy. A youth whose heart leaps before the image of a brave man risking his life in a mighty effort to overcome a great visible danger, is more likely to act the hero himself when the occasion comes than one whose soul is dead to all sense of heroic feeling.

But there is a wide difference between heroes. Some wicked men are heroes. Like that famous admiral, Lord Nelson, they have natures that never know what it is to be afraid. A bad or mean motive suffices to lead such men to acts of wonderful daring. But their heroic deeds, lacking a good and lofty motive, cannot be called noble. They only are noble-minded heroes who choose to risk health, property, prospects, and life as acts of love to the divine Jesus, done for the good of other men. These are moral heroes, and of more such morally heroic souls I will now proceed to tell you.

Imagine a young man, pale and sad, moving with feeble steps down the aisle of a Methodist Episcopal Church in Norfolk, Virginia. An Annual Conference is in session there, with Bishop Hedding, now of precious memory, in the chair. The young man quietly seats himself among his brethren, exciting no higher feeling than pity. They know that he had been called to follow the remains of a beloved wife to an early grave, that his health is so much broken that he has been forced to quit his charge and travel as an invalid in the farther South. But they see not that the flame which lights his eyes is a radiation from the missionary fire which is burning with an unquenchable blaze within his throbbing breast. Yet it is even so.

At a proper hour this delicate invalid sought an interview with the venerable Bishop Hedding, to whom he opened his heart freely, and said: "I desire very much to be sent as a missionary to South America."

"Why not go to Liberia?" asked the Bishop, who had been vainly trying for some time past to find a man willing to go to Africa.

Liberia! That was a land of fatal fevers and probable early death. It was an infant colony, formed of freedmen sent out by the Colonization Society, that they might grow into a community which, perchance, might become a light to the benighted tribes of interior Africa. The Bap tists had already sent out one white missionary, named Calvin Horton, who had already fallen a martyr to the deadly coast fever. Was the missionary fire in this invalid's breast sufficiently strong to incline him to say "Yes" to the Bishop's question?

It was. This youth, whose name was Melville Beveridge Cox, had the soul of a moral hero, and therefore, after a thoughtful pause, he finally replied:

"If the Lord will, I think I will go."

Of course this grandly heroic youth knew that by this answer he was in all probability signing his own death-warrant. Had he been less consecrated to his Master than he was, reflection on the perils of his proposed mission would have cooled his ardor, and possibly have moved him to change his purpose. But, like all truly noble souls, he thought not of himself, but of the work he might accomplish for the poor freedmen who were struggling with the difficulties of settlement in a new home in a sickly climate. Hence, after a short time given to reflection, he said of himself, "Liberia is swallowing up all my thoughts."

As soon as suitable arrangements were made for his support by our Missionary Society he was duly appointed to the Liberia Mission. Thus the die was cast. Did he shrink now that he stood face to face with his perilous work? Not he. On the contrary, he was exultant as one who enters upon a rich inheritance. See him with radiant face sitting, writing to a friend, and saying,

"I thirst to be on my way. I pray that God may go with me there. I have no lingering fear. A grave in Africa shall be sweet to me if he sustain me."

This beautiful passage from one of his letters shows that he expected to lay down his life for the good of Africa. Perhaps the shadow of the Destroyer was already falling upon him. Perhaps he looked upon himself as a needed sacrifice to be laid on the missionary altar for the good, not of Liberia only, but also of the countless hosts of degraded beings which occupy that

Dark Continent men call Africa. What but this truly sublime thought led him to say to a friend about that time:

"I know I cannot live long in Africa, but I hope to live long enough to get there; and if it please God that my bones shall lie in an African grave, I shall have established such a bond between Africa and the Church at home as shall not be broken until Africa be redeemed."

In the same self-sacrificing spirit, when visiting Wesleyan University, at Middletown, Connecticut, he said to one of the students:

"If I die in Africa, you must come over and write my epitaph."

"I will," the young man replied; "but what shall I write?"

"Write, *Let a thousand fall before Africa be given up?*" was his grand response. Never were nobler words spoken by mortal man since Paul stood with the cruel sword of Nero flashing upon him, "ready to be offered" as one of his Lord's martyrs.

The first practical test of his high purpose

was reached when the day of his embarkation arrived. He had expected to have a companion to share his perils and labors, but her courage failed her, and he had to start alone. Then he had to bid adieu to the graves of his sainted wife and child, to his personal friends, to the Church, and to his native land. The trial was indeed a sore one, especially in view of his premonition of impending death. But, like a genuine hero, he never faltered. "I feel a little sadness," he said, very frankly. Sadness under such circumstances was human, but his unshrinking faith and his hope of what the gift of his life might accomplish for Africa were divine—the work of that indwelling Comforter whose presence was the inspiration of his sublime heroism.

He commenced his memorable voyage on board the "Jupiter," November 6, 1832. Sea-sickness prostrated him. Unusually severe storms rudely tossed the uncomfortable vessel, and head-winds prolonged his passage; but none of these things unbraced his firm spirit, or diverted his thoughts from his chosen field. Amid the violence of the wind-swept ocean he wrote, "Liberia seems sweeter to me than ever." When in mid-ocean his mind was busy planning mission-house, school, church, and farm. Hope's bright dreams showed him young converts, churches, circuits, stations, and conferences in Liberia. As his bark neared the land of his anticipations, his longings, like those of Xenophon's ancient Greeks when nearing the sea, grew into impatience. He strained his eyes to catch a glimpse of its shore. And when it became dimly visible from the deck of the "Jupiter," his enthusiastic words were,

"I have seen Liberia, and live! It rises up as yet like a cloud of heaven!"

He landed at Monrovia on the 7th of March, 1833. With a zeal like that of Peter, and with Paul's unresting energy, he entered at once on his work. He preached, purchased a mission-house, brought the people into harmony with his plans, improved the Sunday-schools, held a camp-meeting, visited the colonists at their homes, marked out suitable places for missionary occupation, secured a church lot, and so filled his mind with conceptions of the needs of poor Africa, that his heart yearned with inexpressible desire to see the saving truths of the Gospel taught to her millions of degraded children. Less than four months of this enthusiastic work and holy emotion passed before the deadly coast fever laid its burning hand upon him. But when it touched him it was with the finger of death. On the 21st of July he awoke from a torpid slumber, cried, "Come, come, come, Lord Jesus, come quickly!" and then ascended to Paradise. O, happy hero of the Cross! He fell, as he expected, a sacrifice upon the altar of Africa's redemption. He had his reward in heaven, but his heroic soul still lives on earth, giving inspiration to the missionary spirit of our Church, which is girdling the world with missionary Churches.

But before Cox had passed into the celestial life his example, unknown to him, had moved five others of like spirit with himself to risk their lives for the good of Africa. Their names were Rev. Rufus Spaulding, Rev. Samuel O. Wright, their wives, and Miss Sophronia Farrington. Their self-devotion was put to a severe test before leaving home by the sad news of the death of their heroic leader. But their courage, being born of heavenly love, kept them undaunted, and they cheerfully sailed in the "Jupiter" in November, 1833. On their arrival they organized the "Liberia Annual Conference." Their hopes of usefulness were growing bright, when, alas! after only one brief month, the fatal fever that had slain Cox swept Mrs. Wright into an untimely but glorious grave. Some six weeks later the same cruel disease set the soul of Mr. Wright free from its house of clay, and sent it to occupy "a house not made with hands, eternal in the heavens."

Mr. Spaulding, also finding himself disabled by fever, concluded to return to America. Miss Farrington, being unlikely to recover from the same disease, he proposed to take with him. At first, her case seeming to be hopeless, she consented. But when a renewed attack came on, and the doctor, after pronouncing her death certain and near, had left her with only a native girl asleep in her room, she, in her heart-agony and loneliness, exclaimed, "Is there not some one to sympathize with me?" For a moment she was in the depths. But her precious Lord, who had himself known the grief of being left to suffer alone, came to her help. He revealed himself to her heart, caused her to believe that she ought to remain in Africa, and moved her to pray, saying, "Then, Lord, remove this disease." Instantly her fever left her. The prayer of faith had triumphed, her courage revived, her body was healed.

Presently her doctor came back expecting to find her dying or dead. Seeing her alive and well, he gazed on her with astonishment, and said:

"Well, yours is the greatest cure I have ever accomplished."

Miss Farrington knew that it was not he, but the Great Physician, who had healed her body;

but she said nothing, not wishing, perhaps, to deprive him of the satisfaction he felt over her case.

Mr. Spaulding soon called to talk of preparations for their return to America. Since their arrival eight missionaries of different denominations had died. Spaulding was, therefore, led to believe that Africa could not be saved by white missionaries. But this noble lady said:

"No; I can never see this mission abandoned. I can die here, but I will never return until this mission is established."

Spaulding's gentle nature was touched. He could not endure the thought of leaving this heroic woman to fill another missionary grave, as he no doubt believed she would. Hence he replied:

"But the Board will probably cut you off if you do not return with me."

"I will stay and trust the Lord," was her truly grand rejoinder.

Mr. Spaulding and his wife returned home to recover as best they might from the enfeebling fever which forbade their longer stay. But the brave Sophronia remained alone, the only white person on the coast of Liberia. The same divine fire that had burned in the heart of Cox was giving warmth and zeal and heroism to her finely touched spirit. Never did woman of ancient or modern fame give expression to a loftier sentiment than did this accomplished lady when she said:

"I am ready to offer my soul upon the altar of my God for the salvation of Africa!"

This was no idle speech, no vain boast, uttered in a moment of excitement, but the genuine expression of a spirit consecrated wholly to the Master's most severe and perilous work.

A few months after Mr. Spaulding's return, another missionary, destined to win immortality in missionary history through his great work in Liberia, landed in Monrovia. His name was John Seys. The only white person he found to greet him on his arrival was this persistent heroine—the sole representative of the first band sent out by our Missionary Board. Emaciated, pale, and feeble in person, yet strong of heart, firm in faith, and cheerful in feeling, Miss Farrington bade him welcome to that land of death. How he felt one may partly judge from these words of Mr. Seys:

"Never will I forget my first emotions as I first took the hand of, and was welcomed to Africa by, the only representative of the Methodist Episcopal Mission in that country, and that representative a delicate, frail, emaciated woman."

Miss Farrington kept her resolution to remain in Liberia until the mission was established. The judicious labors of Mr. Seys soon accomplished this result. And then this elect lady returned to her native land. She subsequently became the wife of Mr. George Cone, of Utica, New York, happy, doubtless, in her consciousness that she did what she could for the Lord in Africa, and honored by all who know how to appreciate Christian heroism in a noble woman.

We can afford space for brief sketches of only two more of the heroic souls who placed their lives on the missionary altar in our Liberian Mission. John Seys, mentioned above, was a native of Santa Cruz, in the West Indies. He had spent most of his life in those islands. He owed his conversion to the labors of Wesleyan missionaries from England, and was laboring as a missionary to the Oneida Indians in New York. Bishop Hedding wrote asking him, "Will you go to Liberia? Your birth and early life in a climate so nearly like that of the African coast may have fitted you to resist the fever which has proved so fatal to our lamented Cox." Seys read this letter to his wife. Did she bid him refuse the Bishop's offer? Nay. Did she refuse to go with him? No, no. The love of Christ in her heart had given her so much of her Lord's self sacrificing spirit that she replied:

"I am willing to accompany my husband wherever God and the Church see fit to send him."

These words, so beautifully expressive of conjugal tenderness and womanly heroism, are worthy to be written in letters of gold. They were decisive in her husband's case. He consented to go to Africa, and the notes of preparation for the perilous enterprise were heard immediately in their little household, and in our Mission Rooms at New York. Just then Mr. Spaulding arrived, bearing the sad tidings of the deadly ravages of the African fever recorded above. His words shocked the Church. The missionary authorities very naturally asked:

"Ought we to send another family into the jaws of death?"

Bishop Hedding wrote to Seys, saying, "I will release you from your appointment if, in view of the recent loss of life in the mission, you so desire."

What an opportunity to escape a deathly peril! Had the noble-hearted Seys had a particle of moral cowardice in his heart, he would have seized it with avidity. But he was throughout a man of heroic mold, and, with justifiable scorn, he refused to give up a work to which he now felt that God had called him.

Hence he sailed in September, 1834, but had

to do so without wife or children. Sickness compelled that heroic lady to remain behind. This added heart agony to the peril of death. But Seys, braced by faith and hope, accepted this unlooked-for test of his missionary devotion, and crossed the stormy Atlantic with only a young colored preacher, named Francis Burns, for his companion. On reaching the port of Monrovia the first news that greeted him was of more death. Two more Presbyterian missionaries had fallen, a third was sick, and the governor of the colony was in a like condition. What did Mr. Seys say to these discouraging facts? Mark his manly words:

"This was sad news," he wrote; "but this was no time for our courage to fail us."

Surely not; yet nothing less than the highest type of heroic faith could have kept him hopeful in presence of such grim facts. Nor were these the only sad greetings he had to meet. For, after landing, the pale face, sunken cheeks, and feeble steps of the strong-hearted Miss Farrington, the sole survivor of the Methodist missionary band which had preceded him, told him what the invisible pestilence of the place might be waiting to inflict on him. Still more suggestive was the thought, while resting on his couch that night, that he was lying on the same bedstead on which the lamented Cox had ceased to breathe. Surely these things were gloomy enough to sadden any but a noble mind. Did they dishearten our missionary? Read what he said of this first night in Liberia, spent on the bedstead of his predecessor, and then judge. Writing of himself and of young Burns, who slept in the same room, but on another bed, he said:

"Sweet and refreshing rest was soon vouchsafed to us, and it was as sound and as safe as though we had been in a palace in Europe!"

It must be a true and mighty faith that can sleep as sweetly as a happy child in its mother's arms on another's death-bed in an air laden with invisible germs of fever. Well, Seys had that faith. And it kept him not only free from the fear of death, but active also in the service of his Lord. The deadly fever assailed, but did not kill him. He lived to do a blessed work for Methodism, for the Christ, and for Liberia. But the limits of this sketch do not permit me to finish the story of his devotion and success.

The name of ANN WILKINS must not be left out of this brief record of the early workers in our Liberian mission. This heroic lady was born amid the mountains of the Hudson, near West Point. When fourteen years of age she gave herself to the service of her Lord. Five years later she became a teacher of the young, to whom she taught not only the way into the temple of human knowledge, but also to the experience of divine truth. When thirty years old she heard the thrilling story of our mission work in Africa, told by one who had been in that field of sacrifice and death. Her great heart swelled with desire to bear a part in the perils of that mission, and she sent a note to Dr. Bangs, then Missionary Secretary, containing these noble words:

"A sister who has but little money at

command gives that little cheerfully, and is willing to give her life as a female teacher if she is wanted."

Such grand spirits are always wanted where dangerous work is to be done in the wars of Christ's kingdom. Hence, a few months later, she was sent with others to combat both with the angel of death and the spirit of evil. The sight of the palms on the Liberian coast filled her soul with hope, albeit she knew that the pestilential fever lurked beneath their shadows.

Her feet scarcely touched the soil before she began to teach the dark-faced children, and thus to prepare the way for a "Female Boarding School," in which she was to reign after a time as a queen of light and love. Of course the deadly fever soon laid her low; but her strong constitution withstood it, and she recovered. A second time that enemy of life assailed her and bore her again to the brink of death. Then her fellow-workers, despite her protests, insisted on her return to her native land. She yielded. On her arrival, the missionary authorities, seeing her wasted form, believed that her African work was finished. But her undaunted spirit would not succumb; and when three other devoted young women resolved to give themselves to the African mission, she went with them to watch over and guide them until they were acclimated and fairly established in their work.

Two years more of suffering and toil in Liberia compelled her to quit the work she so fondly loved. The voyage and her native climate so far restored her, that she entered the Juvenile Asylum of New York as one of its active officers. But she only went there to die. Six days of sickness in that institution bore her to the gate of heaven. But they were glorious days to her, for the light of her coming bliss so glorified her, that she appeared to her astonished attendants more like an angel of God than a dying woman. The glory of her death was the beginning of her endless life. O, blessed missionary! O, heroic woman! Great is thy reward in heaven.

CHAPTER III.

A PLOWMAN'S HEROIC ZEAL.

"The meal unshared is food unblessed,
Thou hoard'st in vain what love should spend,
Self-ease is pain, thy only rest
Is labor for a worthy end."—WHITTIER.

IT was a memorable day in the life of Elisha, the son of a wealthy Oriental land-owner, when the prophet Elijah found him plowing in his father's field. Busy with his large team of twelve yoke of oxen, the young farmer probably had no thought that a great change in his life-work was so close at hand. It may be that his young heart had often swelled with desire to do something great for God and his country, but as yet no door had opened in that direction, and he had wisely remained at his post, doing the duties nearest his hand and waiting for Heavenly direction.

He had now reached his last day of waiting.

God's messenger, the grave, the stern, the heroic Elijah, enters the field, passes the long team consisting of twelve yoke of toiling oxen, and approaches Elisha, who was guiding the pair next the plow. Then, without saying a word, the prophet casts his mantle upon the young man's shoulders.

How did the young plowman know that by this silent act Elijah was God's messenger, calling him from farm work to the high office of a prophet? He knew it because he felt the breath of the Unseen One upon his soul, moving him to follow Elijah, and giving him an inward anointing for the prophetic work. It was the critical moment of his life. But he was loyal to the God of Israel, and, after kissing a long farewell to his father and mother, and preparing a repast for his father's servants and neighbors, he followed Elijah. As you know, he soon became Elijah's successor, and a faithful wonder-working prophet among his people.

By different means, yet by the same inward voice, did the God of missions call a **young** plowman of modern times into the work of preaching his Gospel to the Chinese. The name of this young tiller of the soil was GEORGE PIERCY. He was born in Yorkshire, England. About thirty-three years ago this young man gave himself to Christ and joined the Wesleyan Church. Like all true disciples, he thought much about the heathen in distant lands. While following his plow his mind drew pictures of the countless millions who were suffering much misery because of the ignorance and idolatry in which they were reared. He heard much at that time of the Chinese, whose land, long shut up against the feet of foreigners, had lately been thrown open to the missionary. He knew that the Wesleyans were a missionary people; that they very much wished to send men to China, but could not, because of the great number of men they had lately sent to other parts of the globe. The more he thought of China, the more his heart burned with desire to go thither himself. Day after day, as he plowed or sowed, this desire grew hotter and hotter. At last, as Elisha felt the glow of Heaven's call when Elijah threw his mantle on his shoulders, so George Piercy one day heard a still, small voice in his heart, calling him to go to China, and to tell its inhabitants the sweet old story of the love of Christ.

It is not always safe to listen to voices in the heart. It is easy to mistake one's own fancies for God's voice. Yet, when a secret whisper in the soul is followed by larger faith, warmer love, and stronger desires to live a good and pure life, it must not be altogether disregarded. If it really be God's voice it will soon find an echo in other minds, drawing their attention to the person called to do some special work for the Lord.

Young Piercy was so sure that God's voice was speaking to him that he quitted his place, which, perhaps, was not a wise thing to do, and visited a friendly gentleman, named Reed, who lived thirty miles away. To him, among other things, he said:

"Mr. Reed, I have an impression that it is my

duty to go to China and tell the people about Jesus."

"The language of the Chinese is not easily learned. China is a long, long way off. You will have very great obstacles to overcome when you get there. You had better go to some less difficult field," replied the cautious Mr. Reed.

But to this and all other arguments, young Piercy meekly, yet firmly rejoined: "I believe, sir, that God has called me to labor in China. I have no such impression that I have a call to any other part of the mission field."

Yet, notwithstanding his firmness, Mr. Reed opposed his plans so strongly, that, at the close of their interview, young Piercy said:

"Well, sir, I will give up my idea, *at least for the present.*"

His partial submission to the judgment of a man every way superior to himself was praiseworthy. It was certainly proper to wait awhile, though still keeping his purpose to be loyal to his impression if it should finally prove itself to be from God.

Once more young Piercy wrought diligently at his farm work. But neither the joyous shouts of the reapers at the harvest-home, nor the stroke of the thresher's flail on the hard floor in winter, could prevent him from hearing that still, small voice which, with increasing emphasis, continued to bid him go to China. Through six months it kept speaking in the inmost chambers of his soul. And then, feeling sure that it was his duty to obey it, he paid another visit to his friend Reed, to whom he said, very modestly:

"The impression on my mind regarding China not only continues, but it is deeper than ever, sir."

After some conversation, Mr. Reed, satisfied that his visitor's convictions of duty could not be rooted out, and that he was resolved to follow them, gave him a letter of introduction to the Rev. William Arthur, one of the Secretaries of the Wesleyan Missionary Society.

Armed with this friendly missive our resolute plowman trudged to London, saw the amiable and large-hearted Secretary, told his story, but gained no encouragement. The Society had no money which could be used at that time to commence a mission in so vast an empire as China.

Was the young man discouraged? Did he begin to think that he was mistaken, and that it was his own, and not God's, voice that he had heard whispering so long in his soul. No, no! He was neither disheartened nor doubting. He seems to have had the faith of a saint and the courage of a hero. Hence, he took the little sum of money he had saved out of his wages, paid the price of his own passage, and sailed for China, without the promise of help from any human being. Like Abraham of old, he went forth not knowing precisely whither he was going, nor how he was to get bread to eat in a strange land and among a people of strange speech.

When about to sail he wrote to his friend Reed, telling him what he had done. Very likely the gentleman shook his head over that letter, and said in his heart that the young man was acting unwisely, that he had more zeal than wisdom. And he was unwise if the voice in his heart was not from heaven; but if it was, then he was acting a grand and noble part. He was calmly facing hardship, danger, possibly death, for his Master's sake. He was bravely placing himself on the altar of humanity, willing to be a sacrifice if so be he might bring a few Chinese idolaters to sing the praises of the Christ he loved. O noble-souled George Piercy! O true missionary of the cross!

What this devout hero felt while on his long wearisome voyage, what fears, what hopes he had, I do not know. Being a man, he must have had, some dark, dreary moments of doubt and depression. But being a true, loving disciple, strong in his conviction that he was in the path of duty, there is no reason for doubting that his sunny hours were vastly more numerous than his cloudy ones. The smile of Christ within his soul, and the star of hope beaming from his sky, kept him happy and cheerful.

Let us join him on the 30th of January, 1851, as he stands on the shore at Hong-Kong, a small island in the mouth of the Canton River, China. The scene is not inviting. The island is mountainous and barren. It is a British colony, but most of its 32,000 people are Chinese. There is no friend there to greet our young missionary. He has but little money on which to support himself. No wonder he stands gazing around with his heart beating hard in his bosom. What can that poor friendless stranger do? He scarcely knows. Yet he has one straw on which to build a hope of finding friends and an open door. What is it? Nothing but a bit of information gleaned in England, that among the British soldiers stationed in Hong-Kong, there is a Sergeant Ross and a few praying Wesleyan soldiers. "I will find Sergeant Ross," he says to himself; and then, after inquiring his way to the barracks, he enters, and says to the first soldier he meets:

"Can you tell me where I can find Sergeant Ross?"

"He is dead!" is the man's reply.

Poor Piercy's heart almost dies too. For a moment his head swims, his nerves are unstrung, and his tongue falters, as he inquires into the particulars of the sergeant's death.

"He was a young man but an old Christian," said the young soldier, with much feeling. "He was the center of a little band of six or seven who sought to save their souls. They often met in his room. But he died, as did some of the other. The rest became indifferent. I have often longed and prayed for a religious companion."

These words from the soldier, whose dress told that he was a corporal in his regiment, were to Mr. Piercy what the sight of an oasis is to the traveler in a desert. He had found a Christian brother who could at least understand his motive in coming to China, and who, though poor and without social influence, might be the first link in a chain of providences leading him to success in soul winning. It took but a little while to bring the corporal and the missionary into the sweet fellowship of Christian love."

" You had better see Dr. Legge, of the London Missionary Society. He is said to be very liberal in his feelings," said the pious corporal, after hearing Mr. Piercy's story.

So to Mr. Legge's house they went together. Finding that gentleman not at home, but preaching in the Chinese chapel, they went thither and listened to his sermon. At the close of the sermon the corporal introduced Piercy to the doctor, who, after hearing his brief account of himself, said, very kindly:

"Come to my house; I have a bed at your service. To-morrow will bring us leisure to consider further."

Thus Mr. Piercy found shelter on the first night after his arrival at Hong-Kong. He also found something more than a lodging. For when he opened his heart to Dr. Legge, that noble missionary also opened his heart to the unknown stranger, and said:

" Do nothing rashly, Mr. Piercy. Look

around. Watch prayerfully for the moving of the cloud of providence. After ten or twelve days, perhaps, you will see your way. In the meantime you are welcome to a bed and the room you have been in, in this house."

This was, indeed, generous treatment. No wonder Piercy said: "I thanked God and took courage." It looked as if He who had called him to China was opening a way by which he might attain the ends of his coming.

Mr. Piercy was no dreamer. He did not sit down in Dr. Legge's house and wait for something to happen. He looked for an opportunity, and finding a room that would hold some sixty persons, he hired it, and began preaching to the English soldiers. He also visited the military hospital. He took lessons in medicine from Dr. Herschberg with a view to using his knowledge for missionary purposes at some future time. God blessed his labors among the soldiers and their wives, and he soon had a little society of twenty souls. These gave good proof of their piety by contributing from their poverty to the support of their heroic minister, whose little store of money was soon exhausted. Besides their help, his friends in England, having heard of his departure, sent him small sums; so that he was able to give his whole time to the work he loved, instead of taking some business position, as he feared, when he started, he should be forced to do. Thus, you see, God was faithful to this good man whom, by a special call of the Spirit, he had sent into China.

It was not to enlightened Englishmen, but to blinded heathens, that Piercy had a mission. Still feeling this call, he decided, after a few months very usefully spent both in preaching and in the study of the Chinese language, to quit Hong-Kong and go to Canton. Once in that great city, he could stand on the veranda of his temporary home and see spread out before him the homes of nearly five hundred thousand heathen souls. This spectacle made him sad. It also made his heart swell with burning desire to go in and out among them, talking to them in their own tongue of Jesus and his wonderful love. And this desire stirred him to constant study of their language, to the daily circulation of Christian tracts and Bibles in Chinese, and to preaching, through an interpreter, to a small congregation of natives, whom he soon gathered in a hired room.

Mr. Piercy soon found that a missionary to the heathen needs much patience, great courage, and mighty faith in the words of Christ. As when one wishes to blast a very hard rock, he must first slowly drill a hole for his powder, so must the missionary toil hard for a time before he can even win the attention of heathen souls. They seemed to say to him:

"Your doctrine is good for foreigners, but it is of no use to us. We have our own sages. Jesus is a sage of the West. Let the foreigners follow him!"

Yet he found some of them willing to take Christian books and tracts. A few would sometimes ask him questions, through his interpreter, in his preaching-room. This encouraged him to keep up his study of their language, and to look with desire for the day in which he should be able to preach to them without an interpreter.

Meantime his noble example was working on other minds in England in favor of China. A student in the Wesleyan Theological School was so moved by it that he stood ready to join him without any promise of support from the Missionary Society. Another young minister caught the same spirit. Both applied to the Secretaries, begging to be sent out. At the same moment, almost, a liberal Wesleyan layman became so deeply interested for China that he offered five thousand dollars down on the day that two missionaries should sail to join Mr. Piercy, and thenceforth to give five hundred dollars per *annum* for the support of the mission. Other hearts were also stirred to offer gifts for the same purpose. These signs of God's working in behalf of China encourage the Missionary Committee. After due consideration they adopted Mr. Piercy as their missionary, and sent out William R. Beach, Josiah

Cox, and Miss Wannop, a trained teacher, to assist him.

Thus, you see, Mr. Piercy's loyalty to the voice of the Holy Spirit not only led him into the Chinese mission-field, but also became a principal cause of the founding of a Wesleyan Mission in that most thickly populated of all lands. Impressions, as observed above, are not usually safe guides to duty; but in this good man's case his success seems to prove that his remarkable impression was not the birth of an idle fancy, but a veritable call from the God of missions.

CHAPTER IV.

ON THE BANKS OF THE GAMBIA RIVER.

"He who plowed and who sowed is not missed by the reaper:
 He is only remembered by what he has done.
Not myself, but the truth in life that I have spoken,
 Not myself, but the seed that in life I have sown
Shall pass on to ages; all about me forgotten,
 Save the truth I have spoken, the things I have done."
—Horatius Bonar.

LET us imagine ourselves in the city of London at the Wesleyan Mission House in Hatton Garden, where it stood some fifty years ago. It is a chilly October morning and we are sitting before a blazing coal-fire listening to a number of young men who are candidates for missionary fields. A rapping on the outer door is heard. It is opened, and a negro girl bearing a poor sickly white child in her arms is ushered into the room. Who is she? What does she want?

Her story is simple and very sad. She is the child's nurse. The little one is fatherless and motherless. His father, a Wesleyan missionary, named Marshall, had died on the banks of the Gambia not long before. His mother, with this nurse and her infant child, had sailed for England a few days after the burial of her beloved husband, and arrived safely at Bristol. But enfeebled by the deadly fever which had robbed her of her husband, and filled with grief at her loss, she, too, had passed into the land of the eternal some forty-eight hours after touching the soil of her native land. This colored girl, the child's nurse, had hastened to London and now, with many tears, she tells this sad story to the Missionary Secretaries and the young men who were waiting to enter upon mission work.

Had those aspiring youths been self-loving sinners this tale of death and sorrow would have made them say, "Don't send us to Africa!" But they were not selfish. The love of Him who left heaven to seek and save the lost had been poured into their noble hearts. Their highest aspiration was to please him and do his work. Hence one of them, named William Moister, was moved to brave the prospect of speedy death and to say, in the spirit of the loftiest heroism, "Here am I, send me to the mission on the Gambia!"

So many Wesleyan missionaries had died in Western Africa that, to succeed them, was like walking into the open jaws of death. The heroic young Moister was engaged to a young lady who had promised to be his bride. Would she consent to go with him to that land of death? She did consent, for she, too, was made of noble stuff. So they were married, sailed for Africa, and in due time arrived at the island of St. Mary's, in the mouth of the Gambia River.

The mission converts soon heard that a missionary and his wife were on board the brig. They gathered along the shore to greet them. Some of them rushed into the water when the boat which bore the missionary and his wife neared the landing place, and carried them ashore in their arms. There a crowd of negroes gathered about them weeping for joy. Kissing the hands of the strangers, and fervently saying:

"Tank God, tank God! Mr. Marshall die, but God send us nuder minister."

This was a delightful reception. The place, too, was beautiful. Stately palm-trees gracefully bowed their lofty heads in the gentle breeze. The verdure was deep and rich. The scenery bore no signs that this was a land of death. Our missionaries were also greatly pleased with the situation of the mission house. When they approached it they saw a jessamine in flower at its door-step. Mr. Moister hailed this sweet flower smiling upon them as a good omen. His bride also accepted it as such, though she could not wholly suppress a sigh when the thought that its situation on the door-step was a sign that the hand of death had been its guardian, since, but for the blow which felled the late occupant of the house, the jessamine could not have held possession of the door-step on which it flourished. The thought chilled them both, but prayer and hope quickly restored them to cheerfulness.

They began their work at once preaching to the people and teaching the children. They soon saw fruit of their faithful labor. Many poor negroes sought Jesus. The children quickly learned to read and sew. Better still, many of them also learned to pray. These were the good things for which our missionaries had come to Africa, therefore, like an ancient apostle, they thanked God and took courage.

After a few months Mr. Moister felt that he ought to sail up the Gambia to a trading settlement where he might find quite a number of people to whom he wished to preach Jesus. His wife had to be left at the mission house to take care of the children in their schools. It was not pleasant for her to be thus left among negroes in a sickly place. But God made her heart strong and, though sad in spirit, she bade him a cheerful adieu, and he started on his mission of mercy.

To sail up the Gambia in a little sloop, in a hot sickly climate, exposed when on shore to wild beasts and savage men, was not pastime, but a dangerous adventure. Our missionary did it for his beloved Master's sake, and though it was quite probable he might be killed by wild men or die of fever, yet he started in cheerful mood. After one day's sail and a night on shore, he stopped at a place where the people, thinking he might be a slave stealer, ran away and hid themselves in the woods. They had never yet seen a missionary. He soon won the confidence of some. The others then returned. The children gathered about him, touched his hand, wondered at its whiteness, and asked:

"Is the white man all white? or are only his hands and face of that color?"

He turned up his coat sleeves. After looking at his arm, they clapped their hands gleefully and said to each other, "He is every bit white, We never saw such a fine white man."

But when he spoke to the people about God, they only smiled and said, "White man's religion is good for white man; black man's religion is good for black man." Still, at his request, they listened to a sermon which he preached under a shed through an interpreter.

The next day the heavens suddenly became black. Thunder roared in fearful peals, and flashes of terrific lightning darted from the sky. The wind was awfully violent. The boat was torn from their vessel and they were forced to cast anchor in as safe a spot as they could reach. This was a tornado, the sign of the near approach of the rainy season. It was his first experience of such a storm, but by no means his last.

More painful to our missionary than the tornado was the vileness of the poor people who had been taught by white slave stealers to love rum. As the sloop sailed slowly up the river, canoes paddled by natives constantly shot out from the shore. The cry of their occupants was not for the water of life, but for the fire-water of death. "Mi ma sugar! Mi ma rum!" that is, "Give me sugar! Give me rum!" they shouted. Alas! that men calling themselves by the pure name of Christian, should have gone before the missionary, not to prepare his way, but to make it more difficult to win them to Christ. Yet in spite of all this our missionary, after spending a week or two at a village on M'Carthy's Island, found the people so interested in his preaching as to beg him to come again or to send them a "white minister."

On returning home Mr. Moister found his wife in good health. During his absence, however, she had been both annoyed and frightened by parties of natives who, stopping at the mission house, said, "We have come to pay our respects to the white minister."

"He is not at home," the servant said. "Then," they replied, "we wish to see the white lady."

Afraid to refuse, Mrs. Moister said they might enter the house. Seated on her chair in the middle of the room, she awaited their coming. The door opened. The savage, half-nude creatures filed in, squatted on the floor around her chair, gazing with curious eyes upon her, for she was the only white lady on the island. In their hands they bore spears and war clubs.

Do you wonder that she felt afraid? and that her voice trembled as she asked them,

"Why have you come here? What do you want?"

Their reply was in their native language which meant, said her school-boy interpreter, "We have only come to pay you compliment, ma'am." Then she told them about Jesus and his word, gave them pieces of red cloth, a few needles, and some beads which pleased them. Then thanking her with many bows and grimaces they filed out and returned to their inland homes. Several such parties had visited her during her husband's trip up the river. Their visits tested her courage. But her faith in Him at whose command she had entered on missionary work made her woman's heart strong to endure this and many other trials.

Worse than these savage visitors was the coming of the deadly fever into their missionary home. On a Sunday evening it smote her, causing her blood to course through her veins like liquid fire. Her husband hurried to the doctor of the colony for medical help. What medical skill could do that gentleman did. But the fever fought fiercely for so fair a victim, and the missionary saw his beloved helpmeet sink lower and lower until life seemed almost extinct. Hope was changing to despair when the Master of life touched the fountains of her vital forces with healing hand. She rallied and gradually recovered.

Weary with long watching and wearing anxiety, though glad of heart at seeing his wife well again, our missionary himself was notified by a violent headache, pain in the limbs, and burning heat through his body, that the dreaded fever was about to assail him. With determined effort he struggled against it. Vain contest! He was no match for the powerful coast fever. It took possession of him and drove him close to the realm of death. His wife grew anxious. His physician watched him closely. His negro converts held meetings night after night praying for his recovery. The crisis came. He too rallied and recovered.

This was his first, but not his last, attack of fever. Again and again both he and his wife were smitten low by it. And after they quitted this deadly field of missionary labor each of them could and did say,

> "Oft from the margin of the grave,
> Thou Lord, hast lifted up my head;
> Sudden I found thee near to save,
> The fever owned thy touch and fled."

Scarcely had Mr. Moister left his bed before the hoarse voice of war reached his ears. The fierce Mandingo tribes were in arms. The island of St. Mary, which was their chief mission field, was in danger owing to the vast numbers of the savage negroes and the smallness of the British force which held the island. In the emergency every one was called on to defend the place. Men were armed and drilled, women and children carried stone for the erection of a fort. Even Mrs. Moister and her school girls made sand bags for the erection of movable batteries. The principal fighting was done within sight of the island. The dead and wounded were brought in after every conflict. The noise, bustle, and carnage of war almost broke up the mission schools, and the congregation grew small and irregular. Happily, however, some English vessels of war came to their relief. The Mandingoes were routed and peace once more reigned over the island. Then our missionary resumed his labors with his old vigor, thankful that he and his wife had been brought safely through the distressing perils into which their desire to save lost souls had led them.

In one of his visits to M'Carthy's Island, Mr. Moister could find no place of shelter but a miserable, forsaken hut. He took possession of it, and, having brought a supply of food with him, proceeded, with the aid of his negro boy, to prepare his evening meal. There was no furniture in the wretched hut. Finding an old window shutter near by and an empty flour barrel he placed the former on the latter and thus made a table. An empty bottle served as a candlestick. An old native loaned him "a white man's chair." After eating a frugal supper he sought a place to sleep. The hut was damp and chilly, utterly unfit to sleep in. He went outside and found an open shed in the yard. Seeing an old gate he moved it into the shed, propped it up with stones, spread his mattrass upon it and went to sleep. Awaking in the night he saw in the bright moonlight two or three large lizards crawling very near to him. At first the sight of these disgusting creatures inclined him to get up and drive them away. Then, thinking, "they are harmless," he closed his eyes and went to sleep again. These discomforts were frequent when on his missionary tours, but they did not chill his zeal nor cause him to regret that he was working for Jesus on the banks of the Gambia. Had not Jesus suffered even death for him?

Let us now follow him to a village named Yassow, whither he went one day to visit the Mandingo king, Bruma. The streets round the royal residence are narrow and dirty, the palace (?) is a square tower built of mud. Just inside its door is a rude hall, with various figures on the roughly painted walls. Next to this is a courtyard. Let us pass with Mr. Moister through this yard and into a common mud-walled hut. Here is the sable monarch, not seated on a throne, but reclining on a couch. He is intoxicated, and cannot sit up until helped to do so by his attendants. He cannot say much, but tries to be very polite to the missionary.

After a few minutes, he draws an old English tea-kettle from under his couch. This is his majesty's decanter. It contains rum! See! he places the spout to his lips and drinks freely. Now he pours the fiery poison into a calabash and offers it to the missionary, who, of course, declines to take it. But what do these naked children want who come running into the royal hut? Rum! The king gives them the calabash. They drink heartily. The missionary now explains the object of his coming to Africa. The tipsy king listens with a stupefied gaze and says, in reply, "It is very good." You can easily see however that he cares nothing about it.

The missionary prepares to leave. King Bruma gives him a calabash of honey. His visitor in return gives him several silver pieces. His majesty is not satisfied, but begs for every thing he sees about Mr. Moister's person, even to his penknife. As Mr. Moister bows his farewell and returns to his boat, the thought of this sinful king fills him with disgust; but when he thinks that he and his people are immortal creatures whom Jesus died to save, his heart swells with grief and pity, and he resolves to be more than ever zealous in teaching them the blessed Gospel which he knows, by what he sees every day, is able to make even them wise unto salvation. Christ-like is the spirit of every true missionary!

Two years of hardship, faithful work, and frequent attacks of fever bore Mr. and Mrs. Moister toward the brink of the grave. They had seen nearly a hundred of those degraded Africans made happy in Christ, and had taught numerous children about Jesus. They loved their work, yet felt that they must leave it or die. Other missionaries having come from England to take their places, they bade farewell to their converts, who wept to see them depart. They then took ship for their native land, where in due time they arrived safely. Surely in that day in which the Lord will make up his jewels such disciples as Mr. and Mrs. Moister will be accounted worthy to be numbered among the Lord's most honored servants. And it surely cannot be that so long as men and women willing to endure hardness as they did in mission fields, those who love Christ will not refuse to give the money needed to send them forth with their sickles to help reap in the Lord's harvest fields!

CHAPTER V.

INDIAN VOICES.

"Spread, mighty Gospel! spread thy soaring wings!
　Gather thy scattered ones from every land;
　Call home the wanderers to the King of kings;
　Proclaim them all thy own; 'tis Christ's command."
　　　　　　　　　　　—C. ASHWORTH.

SOME of the grandest rivers on the earth owe their origin to a streamlet so scant that a thirsty ox might drink it dry. In like manner, many of the most important facts in the lives of men and nations are born of words which, but for the power of God, would have vanished like the breath with which they were spoken. In this sketch you may learn how a few words spoken by a rude hunter to some ignorant Indians became the seeds of a most precious harvest.

About half a century ago, a hunter and trapper, while seeking game in the vast forests bordering on the Pacific Coast, fell in with a tribe of Indians known as "Flatheads." They bore this odd name because their foreheads were flattened into an acute angle. Nature did not give them this strange deformity; but it was formed by the custom of the tribe to tightly strap a board upon the head of every infant until it grew permanently into this unnatural shape. Our hunter, when on the hunting-grounds of these people, happened one day to witness some of their religious ceremonies. Whether he felt Christian pity for their ignorance, or was disgusted at the sight of such folly, is not known. But, whatever his motive, he said to one of the chiefs :

"Your worship is all wrong. In the far East the white man has a book which tells about the true God, and how men can worship him aright."

These simple words sank into the hearts of the Indians. One cannot doubt that the Holy Spirit made them things of power, exciting their desire to learn what this wonderful book contained. So, after much talking about what the trapper had said, they sent four of their chiefs across the Rocky Mountains in search of white men who could give them the Holy Book, and teach them how to worship God aright.

The journey was long. Three thousand miles of trackless wilderness, uninhabited except by a few Indian tribes, lay between their native wigwams and the city of St. Louis, whither they bent their steps. True, they were used to life in the wilderness; for food they could kill the animals, with which the forests and plains then abounded. Nevertheless, the length of the journey, the severe storms, the treacherous swamps, the steep mountain passes, the dry, almost waterless, plains, and other hinderances, created hardships and dangers, trying even to Indian craft, skill, and strength. Proof of this was given when, shortly after their arrival in St. Louis, two of those hardy chiefs died, literally worn out by the toils they had endured. Their companions started on their return journey, but whether they ever reached the village of their tribe no man knows. Most likely they perished on the way.

But, though those red inquirers after truth died, their singular mission proved to be a blessing, if not to their own people especially, yet to the country from which they came. In St. Louis they told their story to General Clarke, whom they had seen in their own land when he was on an exploring expedition to the Pacific Coast some time before. The general related the facts to others. They found their way into print. The President of the Young Men's Missionary Society, in New York, learned them. He published their substance in our "Christian Advocate." They might have passed unheeded even there before the eye of our Church had not the Holy Spirit used them as sparks to kindle a holy fire in the heart of one of her noblest minds. When that paper reached the study of Dr. Wilbur Fisk, President of Wesleyan University, Middletown, Connecticut, and that man of blessed memory read of the four Flathead chiefs and their venturesome journey, his heart leaped with wonder and joy. He seized his pen and wrote an article bearing this stirring title:

"Hear! hear! Who will respond to the call from beyond the Rocky Mountains?"

His article sounded through the Church like the blast of a trumpet summoning an army to battle. It called for men with the heroic spirit of martyrs to go to the Flathead Nation. "Were I young and unincumbered," said the great-hearted scholar, "how joyfully would I go!"

Nor did Dr. Fisk trust wholly to this grand appeal. He wrote to our Missionary Board with such effect that, in a few weeks, that body requested our Bishops to establish an "Aboriginal mission west of the Rocky Mountains."

The zealous doctor wrote also to Jason Lee, once tutor in Wilbraham Academy, but then a missionary to Indians in Canada. To him he said: "Money shall be forthcoming. I will be bondsman for the Church."

Lee promptly replied, "I will go." His nephew, Daniel Lee, also consented to enter the almost unknown missionary field. Two laymen, named Cyrus Shepard and J. S. Edwards, also agreed to accompany them.

The call of Dr. Fisk communicated his own lofty inspiration to the whole Church, and also to Christians of other names. As Dr. Reid, without the least exaggeration, observes: "All the land was in a flame." Men became eager to give their money to send missionaries to a people who had sent messengers three thousand miles asking for the truth. One young man gladly laid all his property, two thousand dollars, on the missionary altar to be expended in an effort to give light to those inquiring Flatheads. If their messengers had accomplished nothing more than the enkindling of this grand missionary enthusiasm, their long journey would not have been in vain. But though the precise end they sought was not achieved, yet, as we shall see, they were God's instruments for doing a still greater work.

Thus did God move some men to go, and others to give the money to pay the expenses of their journey. But how were they to reach that distant spot? To go by sea, round stormy Cape Horn, implied a dreary voyage of some twenty thousand miles in a sailing vessel. To go by land, as the Indian chiefs had come, was to face hardships such as few besides Indians inured to the privations of savage life, or hunters and explorers hardened by habit and skilled in woodcraft, could endure. To-day our broad continent can be crossed from sea to sea in sumptuous cars; but, half a century ago, after reaching the Mississippi, the journey had to be made afoot or on horseback, slowly, tediously, amid perils of the wilderness, the forest, the desert plain, the wild mountain pass, the swollen river, the rage of wild beasts, and the treachery of the red men of the woods. Our missionaries elect were unused to such hardships and perils. Nevertheless, they had heroic souls, ready to dare for their Lord whatever men could reasonably hope to accomplish. And when a Massachusetts man, named Captain N. J. Wyette, who had previously crossed the Rocky Mountains, consented to act as their guide, they cheerfully turned their backs on pleasant homes and affectionate friends, and plunged into the wilderness on their perilous errand of love.

It would, no doubt, interest you very deeply to learn how this noble little band marched, camped, forded rivers, threaded swamps, ascended mountain roads, endured unusual toils, and lived on food which, but for the clamors of appetites made keen by out-door life, would have been utterly unpalatable. But in a brief sketch like this such details cannot be given. You must, therefore, be content with the statement that, after nearly five months of travel, they arrived, on the 1st of September, 1834, at Walla Walla, near the point where that stream pours its waters into the broad Columbia River, in what is now known as the State of Oregon.

Did they find the Flathead Indians in Oregon? They did, but not in such numbers as they had been taught to expect. They proved to be only a very small tribe. This was a disappointment. But our missionaries met with some other Indian tribes, and with some white men who had been attracted to the territory in search of adventures or gain, or both. Some of these whites were in almost as much need of missionaries as the more ignorant Indians, since they had never heard a Gospel sermon until they listened to these Methodist preachers.

Though disappointed with respect to the number of the Indian population, our adventurous missionaries were not disheartened. They did not, they could not, then know the vast importance of their presence in that beautiful part of our great country. But He who had, no doubt, given secret inspiration to the movements which had led them thither, made them hopeful and courageous. Like men who felt they had a great work before them, they looked for a suitable site for their mission, praying the God of missions to direct them. They finally chose the beautiful valley of the Wallamette, where they built log-houses, and laid up a stock of provisions for the approaching winter. After a time their goods, which had been sent round Cape Horn, arrived. The winter passed. Spring brought with it the necessity of preparing land for crops on which to subsist. They could obtain no helpers, and therefore had to plow, harrow, sow, plant, hoe, and reap with their own hands. This was farming, but it was necessary to the missionary work they hoped to do, since Christ does not feed his servants on manna, as he did the Jews in the Sinaitic desert, but by the usual processes of nature.

You must not suppose, however, that these devoted men gave themselves wholly to farming. Their hearts forbade them to do that. Hence, with longing desire to do their Lord's work, they opened a school for Indian children; they preached as opportunity afforded; they sought for suitable points at which to locate missions among different Indian tribes scattered over the neighboring country. As they pursued their inquiries the prospect for doing good enlarged. They longed to place teachers and preachers among many tribes of red men, and therefore sent home for more missionaries.

The impulse given to missionary feeling by

the visit of the four Flathead chiefs, so eloquently set forth in Dr. Fisk's inspiring call, had not yet died out. Our Missionary Board, therefore, responded by sending large re-enforcements by way of the sea, so that by 1836 no less than twelve adults and three children were added to the four pioneers who had formed the vanguard of this devoted band.

Still the laborers seemed too few for the harvest they hoped to reap. Then Jason Lee said, "I will go to the States for re-enforcements."

Attended by one of his brethren and two Indian boys, Lee started on his return trip across the Rocky Mountains. After a few days' travel messengers overtook him bearing these sad tidings:

"Your wife and her new-born babe are dead!"

The missionary's heart was sorely wounded. Yet, knowing that if he returned he could not look on the now decaying form of her he loved, he pressed on, though with a heavy heart. His presence in the East fanned the missionary enthusiasm of the Church into a flame. Money poured into the missionary treasury, and in October, 1839, the then unexampled number of thirty-six missionary assistants, including preachers, teachers, farmers, and mechanics, sailed for Oregon. Wisely or unwisely, it was thought best to connect much secular work with the spiritual interests of this great mission.

"But what of the Indians?" inquires the reader. "Were many of them saved by those missionaries?"

Many Indians were brought under Christian instruction. How many were actually led to Christ I do not know. Perhaps nothing like the number hoped for by the Church in the States, or by the noble men and women in Oregon. Perhaps the mission was on too grand a scale for the population. Yet it was not either labor or money wasted. Its magnitude, and the peculiar occasion that called it into being, attracted much public attention to the country. Emigrants began to pour into its fruitful valleys. The missionaries, being on the ground, met them with the holy Gospel. Many of them were converted and organized into Methodist Episcopal Churches. Thus the infant State had in this mission a spiritual cradle in which it was faithfully nursed into the possession of a Christian character. The Jesuit priests, whose influence over the Indians is never desirable and who did their best to make the country British, were held in check, and Oregon, largely through the influence of our mission, became American. What it has already accomplished has amply repaid its cost. Its beneficial influence is still working in the life of its people, who have just occasion to thank God for what our Church did in response to the inquiry of the four Flathead chiefs.

Oregon Institute.

CHAPTER VI.

HEROIC WORK AMONG NEW ZEALAND SAVAGES.

> "Which is love?
> To do God's will or merely suffer it?
> I must headlong into seas of toil,
> Leap forth from self, and spend my soul on others."
> —Charles Kingsley.

IN the vast Pacific Ocean there are thought to be not less than ten thousand islands. In this sketch I wish to introduce you to one group of these "isles of the sea," known as New Zealand, which was visited sixty years ago by one of the most heroic men who ever bore the honored name of Missionary. This gentleman's name was NATHANIEL TURNER. He was an Englishman, and a member of the Wesleyan Methodist Church. After enlisting under his Lord's banner he heard a voice in his heart bidding him carry the "good things" of the Gospel to some heathen land. The Wesleyan Missionary Society approved him; but, its treasury being fifty thousand dollars in debt, Mr. Turner was told to wait until money enough could be found to send him out.

About that time a Mr. Leigh, a missionary in New South Wales, who had visited New Zealand for his health, came to England. The sad condition of the New Zealanders had touched his heart, and he implored the Committee to start a mission among them. When he found the Committee had no money, he obtained permission from the Wesleyan Conference to beg articles of manufacture which might be as good as money to missionaries who could barter them among the natives for land, building materials, and food. It was an odd thing to do, yet it succeeded. He begged an immense number of axes, razors, fish-hooks, pots and kettles, with prints and calicoes, and much other goods. These were shipped at once, and a message sent to the waiting Mr. Turner, saying,

"Prepare to go to New Zealand!"

Mr. Turner knew full well that the New

Zealanders were fierce savages, to whom human flesh was the daintiest of dishes. Nevertheless he gladly obeyed this order. And Miss Anna Sargent, to whom he was betrothed, undismayed by the prospect of a long and dangerous voyage, or by the possibility of being killed and eaten by cannibals, consented to become this missionary's bride. And thus it came to pass that on the 3d of August, 1823, this heroic pair landed at the Bay of Islands, New Zealand, where the members of the "Church Mission" received them very kindly. The Wesleyan Mission, the site of which had already been selected by Mr. Leigh, who had begged the pots, kettles, etc., in England, was at a place called Wangaroa, forty miles away.

A schooner carried them and their goods to Wangaroa Bay. It was a romantic spot. The mission house, scarcely yet finished, was in a lovely sequestered valley twelve miles from the harbor. Pine-clad hills and mountains rose in somber majesty behind it, and a winding river, the Kaio, added to the freshness and verdure of the delightfule vale. But, alas for their comfort! it was the rainy season. The roof of the mission dwelling was little better than a sieve. Mr. Leigh was sick. To keep dry he had slept for some time in an empty cask, and he was now forced to leave Wangaroa in the schooner which had brought Mr. Turner, to seek a passage to Van Dieman's Land by the first vessel that might touch at the Bay of Islands. But with three assistant missionaries, Mr. and Mrs. Turner kept up their spirits. After selecting a better site for a mission house, the little band, aided by some hired natives, erected a cottage with a wooden frame which Turner had brought from Sydney.

This necessary task soon gave our missionaries a taste of the treatment they were likely to receive from the savage people they had come to teach. The chief, George, pretended to be friendly at first. After a few days, however, he drove off the native workmen, and said to Mr. Turner,

"That house you are building is mine. I

will knock it down. You missionaries shall go away."

Upon this, three of the dark-eyed, thick-lipped natives seized the spades with which the missionaries were leveling the ground. The furious creatures began to utter loud, savage cries, which were kept up for some time by different parties, both day and night. One day the chief brought Mr. Turner a pig for which he had been previously paid; but he now demanded his pay a second time. Mr. Turner, after some delay, gave him an iron pot he had asked for. This peace-offering, instead of winning, angered him still more. He seized an ax and a frying-pan, and broke the iron pot in pieces against an anvil. Mr. Turner withdrew to a short distance. The chief raised his loaded musket and threatened to shoot him. God's hand restrained the monster. Yet he went near the missionary, half frantic with rage, and pushed him violently round, saying as he did so,

"You want to make us slaves; we want muskets, powder, and tomahawks. You give us nothing but prayers. We don't want to hear about Jesus Christ. If you love us, as you say you do, give us blankets."

After this he went to the house, and said to Mrs. Turner and a white servant-girl she had brought with her:

"I will kill you as I did the people of the "Boyd.""

The "Boyd" was a ship which George and his men had once seized by stealth, and whose crew they had killed and eaten. The chief's threat so frightened the servant-girl that she ran screaming toward Mr. Turner. Fearing that his wife had been murdered, he hastened to the house, where he found her braving the chief with undaunted courage. By and by the fury of this cruel savage suddenly abated. Then, placing his hand upon his breast, he said:

"When my heart rests here, then I love Mr. Turner very much; but when my heart rises to my throat, then I could kill him in a minute."

This outbreak of the chief's rage made the missionaries fully aware that their lives were in momentary peril. No human help was nigh to protect them. But they trusted their Master in heaven, and he kept their souls serene and peaceful.

The next morning Mr. Turner was told that a neighboring tribe had killed a slave, and were about to eat his body. With a courage amounting to rashness, this heroic man, unarmed and unattended, went over the hills and found the chiefs sitting near a large fire. When within their hearing, he asked:

"What are you roasting?"

Looking somewhat ashamed, they were silent while he went to the fire. There, O disgusting spectacle! he saw the slave's body roasting between two burning logs. Seeing his disgust, the chiefs, said by way of apology,

"That man was old and troublesome."

Mr. Turner, aided by his brother missionaries who had joined him, after much talk, succeeded in securing the partly-roasted body and putting it under-ground. It was a daring thing for him to do, since he was completely in the power of men who had never been controlled except by brute force or superstitious fear.

Refusing to be disheartened by the almost daily annoyances and thefts to which they were subjected by those ungrateful cannibals, our missionaries gave themselves to the study of their language. In less than six months they were able to teach children some of the sweet words of Jesus. Within a year they built two Wesleyan chapels with their own hands. They were rough buildings, but they sufficed for preaching-places and for school-rooms. After these were dedicated to the Christ Mr. Turner finished his cottage. While moving into it he was robbed of a case of carpenter's tools, which, after search was made, was found in the hands of a chief named Te Puhi and some of his followers.

Te Puhi, vexed at being caught stealing, led a band of armed followers to the old mission house the next morning. After yelling fiercely outside, they entered the dwelling. One of them seized a bundle of linen. Mr. Turner tried to take it from him, but was struck on his left arm with the flat side of a weapon called a marè. Had the savage used its edge the missionary's arm would have been broken. Fortunately, the old chief, George, in a fit of good nature, came to Mr. Turner's relief, and threatened to kill the man who had struck him if he did not let the missionary alone. Te Puhi's party then left the building and went to the newly-finished cottage. But Mrs. Turner was there with her servant, and she bravely stood at the door and barred them out. That was a day of severe trials to the missionaries, but their faith kept their hearts strong. At evening prayer they thanked God for restraining the savages who, like wild beasts of the forest, had thirsted for their blood. They said, very firmly:

"We will trust in our God, and praise his name for ever and ever."

O noble souls! no wonder that one of the chiefs of the Wangaroa tribes, speaking to a visiting chief of this little missionary band, said:

"We have tried all we could to make them

afraid, but have failed. *They are a courageous tribe!*"

Yes, they had the sublime courage of Christian faith, and among them all not one had a braver heart than the gentle wife of Mr. Turner.

For some months after the dedication of the chapels they were less annoyed. They had good congregations, attentive listeners, numerous children in their schools. Still, not one convert as yet rewarded their diligent labors. By and by a change for the worse came over the spirit of those savages. In March, 1825, Ahudu, a chief, brought an armed band to the mission house, spoke fiercely to Mr. Turner, and brandished his weapon over him as if intending to cut off his head. After a while he and his party left, carrying off a favorite young dog. Missionary White went after them and recovered it. Then Te Puhi, who wanted the dog, set upon Mr. White with his spear. Mr. Turner and Mr. Hobbs ran to his rescue. Te Puhi then assailed Mr. Turner, aiming at his head with his spear.

The missionary received the blow on his left arm. The spear broke. Te Puhi thrust the longest part of the blunted weapon at Turner's side. The good man fell senseless to the ground. By this time Ahudu had thrown missionary White down near the fence. Both would have been murdered in a few moments if some friendly natives had not run up and rescued them. As it was, Mr. Turner was thought to be dead when borne into his house. Happily he recovered, but was so injured by the spear and the shock that it was several days before he was able to leave his bed.

About this time a whaling ship, which put in at Wangaroa Bay, owing to the incaution of her officers, was captured, plundered, and her crew mostly killed. This deed of violence quickened the passions of the natives into a species of madness. It also brought threats of war from a powerful chief at the Bay of Islands, who feared that captains of other ships, hearing of the sad affair, would cease to touch at his port. In that case he would be unable to procure muskets and gunpowder in exchange for supplies of food. And without fire-arms, he would be unable to maintain the superiority of his tribe over other tribes. Hence he wished to punish the tribes at Wangaroa.

This threat of war excited the natives greatly. They vented their rage on the brave Wesleyan missionaries, threatening to seize all their property, and even to kill them. No doubt their spite was made more bitter by fear that a war-ship would be sent from England to punish them for their destruction of the whale-ship. Hence the situation of the missionaries became desperate, and Mrs. Turner and her maid were taken to the "Church Mission," at the Bay of Islands. The noble lady went very reluctantly; but her husband and his associates urged her going so positively, that she finally consented.

Tribal wars and rumors of wars followed, but were of brief duration. Quiet seemed to settle on the Wangaroa tribes once more. Mrs. Turner then returned. Missionary work was resumed. But in January, 1827, Wangaroa was invaded, the natives fled, the mission premises were threatened, and finally assailed by the invaders. The contents were ruthlessly seized, and, when the savages were actually in their dwelling, the missionaries took their departure. As Mrs. Turner was in the door-way, a chief raised his weapon to cleave her to the ground. At that moment some of his followers pushed up a shelf over the door-way and caused a lot of nails stored upon it to fall in a shower upon the head of the chief. This so surprised him that his stroke was arrested, and the heroic lady escaped.

Behold this missionary family! There were Mr. and Mrs. Turner, with their three children, the youngest a babe only five weeks old; two other missionaries, one of them a lady; and a serving man and his wife. All were loaded with bundles of clothing. Their way led across grain fields wet with dew. They had to wade the little, winding valley stream no less than four times. Very soon they met a war party which proved friendly, and let them pass on. A second band of warriors seemed disposed to kill them, and its chief, pointing to the edge of a stream, said, very sternly:

"Kneel there!"

This sounded like their death warrant. But seeing no way of escape they kneeled down, Mr. Turner holding his infant in his arms. Then, to their inexpressible relief, the chiefs came and rubbed noses with them. This they knew to be the symbol of friendship. The chief then bade them "Go onward!" and they moved on into the woods. After walking six miles they were met by friends from the Bay of Islands. By sundown, after a tedious walk of twenty miles, they reached the friendly shelter of the "Church Mission." They had made a heroic effort. Only one convert had been won to Christ. Yet their labor was not in vain.

Before leaving the Bay of Islands for Sydney, Australia, Mrs. Turner, notwithstanding the terrors connected with her flight from Wesley Vale, was loth to quit the field. Yearning with desire to see the bloodthirsty savages changed into meek believers in Christ, and inspired by heroism never excelled, she often said to her husband,

"Cannot we remain and prosecute our mission somewhere in the land?"

This was the language of the heart, and, regarded as an expression of feeling, was both beautiful and sublime. But when the possibility of the situation was viewed in the light of a sober judgment, she saw, as did her husband and associates, that it would be the height of folly to attempt a new mission until a more peaceful spirit should incline those pitiless cannibals to invite their return.

And they did return, though not immediately. After spending six months in Sydney they, with several other missionaries, sailed to the Tonga Mission in the Society Islands. The Tonguese were less savage and warlike than the New Zealanders, but owing to some recent quarrels with the Fijians, had become unusually restless and unteachable. In this state of mind, they had shown such hostilities to the Wesleyan missionaries, had even begun to rob and threaten them so harshly, that when Mr. Turner reached Tongataboo, he found the mission families busy with preparations to abandon the Island. When he told these disheartened laborers that he had come with two other missionaries and their wives to re-enforce the mission, they were greatly astonished. Their good wives, grown nervous through the things they had suffered, when told that three missionary sisters with several children were in the ship waiting to land, expressed themselves in these emphatic exclamations:

"It is madness to bring them here, and subject them to such trials as we have had to endure!"

Perhaps it was madness viewed on its human side. But, placed in the light of faith and duty, it was sublimely heroic. The results justified Mr. Turner and his associates. The God of missions was on their side, and the next few years proved that, as it was with the prophet and his servant at Dothan, they who were with them were more and mightier than the heathenish and Satanic forces arrayed against them.

They met with great success in making converts, and the spiritual beauty of the mission soon became more delightful to the hearts of these noble men and women than the rich verdure, the Eden-like beauty, and the floral brilliancy of the lovely scenery of the Islands were to a mere spectator's eye.

But New Zealand after a few years needed Mr. Turner's return. A change had come over the spirit of its dreadfully savage people. Other Wesleyan missionaries had reaped some fruit from the seed sown by the heroic Turner and his faithful fellow-laborers. Still the field was difficult. A leader of experience was required to guide the workers. Turner was therefore selected to go thither again. It was a great sacrifice of feeling to quit the flourishing societies in Tonga and to return to places where he and his noble wife had endured so many sore hardships. Yet he complained not, because his own sense of duty sustained the voices of authority which bade him make the change.

His wise counsels soon restored vigor to the

workers in the mission. His untiring energy, his strong faith, his superior abilities, quickened the native churches which he found there. There were yet perils to be faced because the enemies of the native churches were many, and the old cruel war-spirit of the New Zealander reappeared at times in some of the as yet partially instructed chiefs who had been baptized. Nevertheless he toiled bravely on, ever pursuing though sometimes faint, until 1839, when, his health being impaired by overmuch toil and by the climate, he sailed with his family to Sydney, Australia. Henceforth his work was among the colonists of that thriving land. His death, in 1864, was more than peaceful; it was triumphant.

New Zealand was greatly blessed by the Gospel, yet many of that warlike race clung to its passion for war, first among themselves, and then with the European colonists who settled there. As the white people increased the dark natives diminished. Nevertheless, in the world of light, many of the missionary converts are doubtless walking in white.

CHAPTER VII.

A SHORT BUT BEAUTIFUL LIFE.

> "If now in youth or when the head be hoary,
>   Earth's ties are riven,
> I know that sudden death is sudden glory
>   To heirs of heaven."

DURING the session of the Wesleyan Conference at Bristol, England, in 1838, a young man with a figure of almost womanly delicacy rose up, and with very deep feeling, said:

"I feel clear that in entering on mission work I am in the path of duty. As a young man in the ministry I have had all my heart could wish; but I feel I must devote myself to the work of God in a foreign land. I know what I am about. I do not expect to escape hardships, privations, and perils. But none of these things move me." Then raising his tearful eyes heavenward, he added, with intense emotion:

> Thine I live, thrice happy I,
>   Happier still if thine I die."

And when the President of the Conference, after a brief reply to this address, shook hands with this young man and his fellow-missionaries, the preachers were so overcome that they wept aloud.

Why did this unusual flood of feeling sweep over that dignified body? Who was the young man whose electric words thrilled them so remarkably? The occasion was the farewell of the Conference to a little band of their brethren about to depart to their missions in the South Pacific Ocean. The young man eloquent was THOMAS H. BUMBY, who, though only thirty years old, had given promise of a grand career in the home ministry. That such a man should turn his back upon the best Wesleyan churches in England to spend his life among such barbarians as the New Zealanders, was a spectacle which filled them with admiring sympathy.

As this noble-minded man was unmarried, his sister, moved by the same heroic spirit, sailed with him, that she might preside over the mission house and aid him in his work. After a six-months' voyage he landed in New Zealand, where Mr. Turner and other missionaries greeted him gladly.

Great changes for the better had taken place in New Zealand since the heroic Turner had been driven from its shores. The good seed had, after a long and perilous sowing-time, found some good ground in which to take root. And on Mr. Bumby's first Sabbath he saw a thousand natives gathered at the missionary station, and preached in the chapel to an overflowing, serious congregation. Surely the Cross had triumphed gloriously!

There was present that day a native teacher, named William Barton, who some time before had been shot at by a party of his countrymen he was trying to instruct. Two of his praying companions were killed outright, and his own blanket was pierced by three bullets. One of the murderers was present that day, and when William Barton was asked to offer the closing prayer after the sermon, he prayed so earnestly, so tenderly, for the guilty man, that the congregation, so recently won from the savage spirit of its ancestry, was deeply moved. To Mr. Bumby that sweet prayer for an enemy was like an angel's song. It revealed to him the mighty power of the truth he had come to preach.

He was also told of a native class-leader, Simon Peter, a chief who had recently died. Of this once-dreaded man one of the missionaries said to Mr. Bumby:

"Simon Peter, before his conversion, was a terror to his enemies. Having taken some prisoners one day in a battle with a hostile tribe, he stopped on his homeward march, made a large oven, heated it, bound his captives, cast them alive into it, roasted, and then made a feast of, their bodies. And yet," added the missionary, "after the Gospel had conquered that terrible man, I often saw the big, scalding tears stream down his tattooed cheeks, while he and his fellow-converts were singing hymns about the love of Christ."

Many stories of the power of Christ's love over the hearts of cannibals increased Mr.

Bumby's faith in the truth, and gave life to his hope that his sacrifices in their behalf would not be in vain.

He soon had occasion to note the quickness of the native mind. Mr. Turner introduced him to a Christian chief, named Nene, saying, among other things, "Mr. Bumby is the father (meaning the superintendent) of the missionaries."

Nene, after looking askance at the frail, slender figure of Mr. Bumby, shrewdly replied: "Ah! it is well: but he a father! He is but a boy; but perhaps he has the heart of a father."

Mr. Bumby, being superintendent of the mission, and under instructions to visit the islands and select suitable sites for new stations, soon found that his anticipations of hardships and perils were not imaginations, but stern realities. He had to travel much by water, in frail native vessels, on seas that were subject to severe storms, and made dangerous by many hidden reefs. Besides being cooped up for days in these unsafe little barks, he had, on landing, to visit the native heathen chiefs, which was often any thing but a safe or pleasant task.

Let us follow him on one of these visits. The chief is a noted warrior and a man-eater. It is his habit to lay his hand upon his stomach and say, in a gruff, imperious voice,

"I am hungry for a man; go and kill ——, a slave, for me!"

The entrance into this chief's house is so low and narrow that our missionary has to crawl on his hands and knees to pass through it. Once inside he finds the air thick with smoke from the oil burners which give the room its gloomy light. Thirty warriors and slaves lie at full length on the floor. The air is so impure Mr. Bumby can scarcely breathe. Yet he stays long enough to sing a hymn and offer a prayer. The next morning this disgusting cannibal visits the missionary on his vessel, and to his surprise says to him:

"Send me a missionary, and I will give over fighting, and begin with all my people to serve God."

Besides preaching and teaching, Mr. Bumby and his fellow-laborers often acted as peacemakers between hostile tribes not yet converted. To do this they often had to make long journeys through dense forests, over rugged mountains, and across vast swamps, during heavy tropical rains and chilling winds. On one peace-making expedition they had to spend a week in such difficult travel, sleeping on beds of fern, with no roof over them but the lofty heaven. This, though severe and perilous to life, was the least dangerous part of their errand of love.

Having reached the seat of one of the warlike tribes, they found the chiefs sitting in state, their persons proudly ornamented with white feathers. To the kind words spoken by the missionaries, they replied with these stern terms:

"We will resist the attack of our enemies to death, to death, to death."

Presently the messengers of the tribe threatening war arrived, demanding satisfaction. This demand excited them to fierceness. They brandished their spears, yelled, and threw so much passion into their faces that they looked more like demons than men. Still the missionaries pleaded for peace, and at last gained consent to go to their coming foes and say to them that, if they would discharge their muskets at a distance, their enemies would meet them as friends.

This was one point gained. To make it effectual, one of the missionaries walked unarmed and alone to face the approaching force. It was like bearding death on a field of blood. But his trust was in Him who had conquered death. The savage chiefs listened to him, and at length agreed, for the missionaries' sake, to meet the opposite party for a peaceful parley.

They then marched, with the missionary at their head, to a hill opposite their enemies' village. In a valley between them, a white handkerchief—the flag of peace—waved from a pole. Mr. Bumby and another missionary stood beside it. On either side the savage warriors stood, nearly nude, armed and ready for strife. The discharge of a single musket, the stepping of a single warrior from either side across the line of peace, would have been the signal for mutual slaughter, in which the missionaries, standing between two fires, must have been the first victims. But those heroic servants of the Lord Jesus did not falter. With faces unblanched by fear, and tongues made eloquent by hearts full of love, they pleaded with the angry cannibals until their fury abated; then they agreed to be friends, fired their muskets into the air, joined in a war-dance with such frantic energy that it made the ground shake beneath their feet. The love and heroism of the missionaries had won a victory over heathen passion which, no doubt, prevented the death of hundreds, and also the loathsome cannibal feast with which the conquering party would have celebrated their victory.

Besides this blessed work of Christian charity the missionaries, by preaching, teaching, and distributing the Scriptures and tracts, were constantly winning disciples for their Lord. In the autumn of Mr. Bumby's first year in New Zealand it was found that over eighteen hundred of those cannibals had been transformed into Christians during the year. Their hunger for the flesh of men had been changed into hunger for righteousness. This grand fact more than compensated those noble men and women for all they had done and suffered. Their Lord had died for this end, and this was the object of their holy ambition.

The great change wrought in these savages by the Gospel was well described by a chief one day, who said:

"Before the missionaries came, we went to all parts of the land to kill and devour our countrymen. My hand was against every man, and every man's hand was against me. I delighted in the blood of others, and never went forth but to scatter, tear, and slay; but since I have heard of Jesus Christ and his Gospel I have desired to publish peace, and have gone to different parts of the land to persuade people to turn to God."

O blessed fruit of missionary labor! It satisfied the heart of the heroic Bumby and of the hundreds of noble-minded men and women who gave their lives to save the heathen during the heroic age of the modern missionary crusade in heathen lands.

The wife of one of the New Zealand missionaries, while moving from one station to another with her husband, in a vessel called the "Triton," was taken with mortal sickness. Her name was Wilson.

"Is it well with you?" one of the missionaries asked her.

Placid as a lake in the bright calm of a still summer's day she replied, firmly, "Yes, it is."

Then, with closed eyes and feeble hands clasped and uplifted, as in prayer, without a sigh or groan or struggle, her happy spirit soared to the glorious presence-chamber of the world's Chief Missionary, the Master of life, the everlasting Saviour. They were compelled to bury her beneath the waves of the Pacific, from whence, in the day of the resurrection, her decayed body will be raised, changed into a spiritual and ever beautiful form.

One more scene, and that a tragic one, must conclude this brief sketch of Mr. Bumby's missionary life. We will join him on board a native vessel sailing from one station to another. Several native converts are with him. It is the month of June, the New Zealand winter. The weather, though cold, is fine as they start. The canoe is overloaded. The crew are careless, and in hoisting the sail to catch a breeze which springs up, the canoe capsizes. The natives, being good swimmers, soon right it, and help Mr. Bumby to get in. To make his person lighter they cut off most of his outer clothing. Shivering with cold, he sits bailing out the water with his hands.

Of course, he now sees himself in peril of death. Yet a little caution on the part of the natives may save both him and them. But they, by crowding back into the frail canoe, upset it again. One of their number sinking before their eyes fills them with panic, and they begin to despair. A converted native, James Garland, helps Mr. Bumby to get astride the upturned canoe. There he holds him. Seeing nothing now but death before him, this delicately formed man calmly, solemnly commits his soul to the Redeemer. The chilly air almost paralyzes him. Presently a swelling wave rolls over the canoe, sweeps him from his perilous seat, and he sinks in the clear, deep water. Fourteen of the others are also drowned. The six who escape do so by righting the canoe and rowing to the nearest shore.

This was in June, 1840. Less than two years had passed since this splendid, sweet-souled preacher's touching farewell to his Conference. Little more than a year of complete devotion to missionary work was permitted him. Was he therefore mistaken in thinking that God had called him to it? Nay, not so. As the martyr's death was the seed from which the Christian Church grew in the ancient days, so the heroism of this beautiful young life, since embalmed in many a missionary speech, has been fruitful in awakening a kindred spirit in others. His work lives also in many a heathen's renewed life.

The tidings of Mr. Bumby's death spread a cloud of sadness over the spirits of the Wesleyan missionaries in New Zealand. His superb pulpit talents had charmed them, his untiring zeal, his rare self-denial, his remarkable piety, and the uncommon sweetness of his meek temper had won their admiration and their love. That such a man should die so early, like a bud of rarest promise rudely broken from its stem, seemed mysterious. Yet, though grieved, they did not doubt either the wisdom or goodness of Him whose providence had permitted him to sink beneath the waters of the ocean. They knew that He doeth all things well.

But how did Miss Bumby, his sister, bear a trial which left her alone in those distant lands? The blow was almost too much for her endurance. Rumors of some mishap reached her at first. Presently a messenger arrived at the missionary station. On seeing him, she eagerly exclaimed,

"Do tell me! do tell me!"

"Your brother is in heaven," her friend replied, very tenderly.

A painful pause ensued. Then the particulars of the catastrophe was told her. Next—words of consolation were gently spoken. She gave them what heed she could, but after some hours her grief threw her into convulsions. A sleepless night succeeded; and then the peace of Christ gained a victory, and her torn heart, though still bleeding, felt that holy calm which always follows submission to the will of God.

Had Miss Bumby been less a heroine than she was, she would have returned to her native land after this great bereavement. But the missionary mantle of her brother had fallen upon her, and she remained in New Zealand to do missionary work. After a time she married a missionary, and, as his faithful wife, did more excellent service in that far off-land.

Mr. Bumby was the first Wesleyan missionary who died in New Zealand. His brethren regarded him as a martyr to the work, but were not discouraged. Theirs was the genuine missionary spirit which, like the old guard of Napoleon, "does not surrender." It was grandly expressed by Mr. Bumby's friend, Rev. John Waterhouse, who two years later died through exposure while doing missionary work. His last words, vehemently uttered, were, "Missionaries! missionaries!"

CHAPTER VIII.

CONQUEST OF BEAUTIFUL TONGA.

> "Dare all thou canst,
> Be all thou darest, . . .
> Have thy tools ready, God will find the work."
> —Charles Kingsley.

IN the vast Pacific Ocean there are three groups of islands, numbering more than one hundred and fifty, called the Tonguese Islands. Captain Cook, celebrated as a navigator, named them the Friendly Islands, because he found their inhabitants less savage than those of New Zealand and Fiji. But, though they treated him with apparent kindness, they were, like all ignorant heathens, cruel at heart, false, thievish, and very vile.

They showed these bad qualities when, in 1797, ten missionary mechanics, sent out by the London Missionary Society in the "Duff," landed at Tonga, the principal island,

and began to preach the Gospel and teach the people useful trades.

At first the natives treated these men very kindly, as they did Captain Cook. But after a few months the chief who protected them was murdered by his own brother. Thereupon war broke out. Three of the missionaries were killed. The others were robbed of their property, stripped of their clothing, driven from their homes, and forced to hide themselves in caves among the rocks, and in desolate places. Reduced to destitution by this cruel treatment, they were glad at length to quit the island in a ship whose captain offered to give them a passage to New South Wales. Thus, you see, the first attempt to lead those Friendly Islanders to the Friend of sinners was a failure.

Yet it was not a final failure. The spirit of the persecuted missionaries was not quenched. It lived long in the heart of a woman, first the wife and then the widow of one of them, named Shelley. This good woman spoke so feelingly of those islanders to a Wesleyan preacher in

New South Wales, named Walter Lawry, that a burning desire to visit them was kindled in his soul. This desire led him to such efforts that, twenty-two years after the enforced departure of the first missionaries, he, with his heroic wife and some assistants, landed at Tonga, and, after a few days, requested the chiefs of the island to meet him.

To this courageous demand seven chiefs responded, bringing with them a vast crowd of their followers, who formed a circle round the undaunted missionary. He told them why he had come to Tonga, and asked them if they were willing to be taught the religion of Jesus.

"Yes," they said. "We will treat you well. We will send thousands of our children to your school."

As if to prove their sincerity, they next made him presents, after the manner of their country. The principal chief went so far as to entreat Mr. Lawry to build a mission house near his abode.

This was, indeed, a sunny beginning. But, alas! it was only as the morning brightness which is sometimes followed by a noontide storm. Those fickle people, after a few short months, changed their tone. When they met to drink *kava* they talked against the missionaries. Said one chief:

"See, these people are always praying to their gods as the other missionaries were, and what was the consequence of their praying? Why, the war broke out, and all our old chiefs were killed."

Another said: "I had a dream. I saw the spirit of an old chief. He was angry because he saw the new mission house, and said the Papalangi will pray you all dead."

These fiery speeches fell upon the people like sparks on gunpowder. They set their bad passions on fire, and moved them to treat Mr. Lawry rudely, to rob him of his goods, and to threaten him, saying in his hearing,

"Make ready! Let us put an end to this Papalangi."

For several months Mr. Lawry stood firmly at his post, enduring their ill treatment with patience; yet knowing, even when they put on the mask of friendship, as they did at intervals, that the fate of the heroic men, "whose graves were before his eyes," might overtake him at any hour. And when the health of Mrs. Lawry made it necessary for her to leave Tonga, as it did after fourteen months of this perilous living, our patient missionary left and returned to New South Wales. As he was about to enter the boat one of the chiefs said, with seeming sincerity:

"We thank you for your visit. We hope you will soon come back."

Mr. Lawry carried away two impressions from Tonga: first, that its scenery was so rich in beautiful trees and flowers, and so flooded with soft sunshine, as to seem more like one's dreams of fairy-land than a part of the solid earth; and second, that its natives, though less ferocious than their neighbors of Fiji, were a vile people living in "islands of peerless loveliness." Nevertheless he pitied them, and, discouraging as the prospect of their conversion seemed, so represented their case that, in 1826, two other Wesleyan missionaries, named Thomas and Hutchinson, landed at Tonga, and fixed their residence at Hihifo. At that time, out of some fifty thousand souls on the islands, not one was found who had ceased to worship the idols of his ancestors.

With their habitual cunning, the chiefs pretended to give Mr. Thomas a cordial welcome. But he soon found that it was not the missionaries, but their property, they desired. Ata, the chief, soon withdrew his protection. Then men, and even boys, insulted them, robbed them, and threatened to kill them.

"They keep boxes of spirits, (spiritual beings,) brought on purpose to eat up the Tonga people," said one of their speakers at a native council.

The chief laughed at this theory. Yet he soon took occasion to disturb the missionaries, driving them from the mission house, and threatening to kill them. He also forbade his people to go to their meetings. He broke up their school, and told them he would not suffer them to buy any thing of the natives. And when a long season of dry weather led them to expect a famine he joined in the popular cry which said:

"The Tonga and English gods have had a quarrel about these missionaries. The Tonga gods are the stronger and are punishing us."

The missionaries were perplexed, even discouraged, seeing nothing but violent death before them. In their extremity they wrote to the Wesleyan authorities in Sydney to send a vessel to take them away from their seemingly hopeless field.

Instead of yielding to this despondent, though by no means blameworthy, wish, the Committee sent them Messrs. Turner, Weiss, and Cross to re-enforce them. They were both surprised and comforted to see these noble helpers. Their hopes revived. A beam of light shone just at that time from a native village, named Nukualofa, where two Christian natives of Tahiti, while on their way to Fiji, had stopped, and had begun teaching the people. These men could not speak in the Tonga tongue, yet their spirit had so attracted the people at Nukualofa, that they began to inquire about Jesus and walk to Hihifo, a distance of twelve miles, to hear the Wesleyan missionaries preach in their own language, either directly or through an interpreter.

Guided by this beam of promise, Messrs. Turner and Cross went on to Nukualofa. Nor did they go thither in vain. They soon had flourishing schools, large congregations, and some serious inquirers, but as yet no real converts.

Nor was their peril wholly ended, as Mr. Turner and his brethren found one day, when going to witness the ceremonies of a great native feast. To get a good view of their sports the missionaries stepped on a mound. A native said:

"That is a burial place. The spot is sacred. You must leave it."

They moved away to a low tree and took seats on its lower branch. The limb broke and they fell. Instantly the club of an angry native was lifted over Mr. Turner's head, while he was yet on the ground. Had the threatened blow been given he would have been a dead man. But the hand of the Unseen One restrained the arm of the heathen, and the missionary was saved. He soon learned that the fierce act of the savage was caused by his belief that the gods were in the toa tree. Fortunately for him, the chief, Tubou, instead of sharing the anger of a man who was the subject of another chief, was enraged with him because he had dared to threaten the life of a man whom he had promised to protect. But when he made a threat of war on the man's tribe unless his chief sued for mercy, the missionaries interfered as peacemakers. It was a critical moment. On the result the fate of the mission probably depended. Happily the spirit of peace prevailed. The offending tribe sued for mercy, Tubou relented, and the mission lived to become a marvelous success.

Tubou's friendship for the missionaries soon

gave offense to the other chiefs. They threatened to make war upon him unless he ceased to approve them. To prevent this the chief prepared to leave Tonga, and go with his people to another island. Had he done so the missionaries would have been obliged to go with him, since to remain would have been certain death. But he finally resolved to stay when the other chiefs, unwilling to lose him, offered to acknowledge him as king of all Tonga. In this they showed their cunning, since they believed that through their submission they could persuade him to turn against the missionaries. A vile hope which, for a time, gave promise of being fulfilled.

The heroic missionary band did not quail in presence of further opposition and persecution. Faith in Christ kept their hearts strong. Love for souls bound them to the poor people they longed to save. They began to receive their reward when, in 1828, they formed ten seekers into the first Methodist class in Tonga, and when, shortly after, a young chief of the highest rank, having found peace through believing, was baptized on his death-bed and died a sweetly Christian death. Hundreds of natives also attended their meetings, and on several of the islands the people grew so serious and attentive that the missionaries rejoiced in hope of brighter days and greater success.

Yet their hour of complete triumph had not fully come. Ata, a chief, was still violent at times. One day he told Mr. Thomas that he must quit Hihifo.

"I shall not leave," replied the courageous man of God, firmly.

"Do you not fear me?" cried the fiery chief, with fury flashing from his eyes.

"No!" replied Mr. Thomas, very calmly. "I do not fear you. I fear no one but God."

Ata, if not awed by this display of Christian courage, was silenced, and the missionaries remained at their post.

The seed sown in tears now began to spring up, promising a joyful harvest. Converts began to multiply. Early in 1830 Tubou, king of

Tonga, stood beside Mr. Turner's pulpit, his manly person neatly dressed in native cloth. With a calm countenance and cheerful voice he said to the crowded assembly:

"The gods of Tonga are vanity and lies. I renounce them. I have cast away all that I know to be wicked. Jehovah is now my God. Jesus is my only Saviour. I this day offer myself, my wife, my children, unto the Lord. I beg you to follow my example, and attend to the things of God."

He then kneeled down, and was baptized by the name of Josiah. After the ceremony he presented his three sons and his daughter to be baptized. In the afternoon of that memorable Sabbath, the greatest priest in Tonga, to whom King Tubou had often prayed as his god, also received baptism. Thus both this royal chief and his god were taken into the Church the same day. O, wonderful victory of the cross! O happy, honored missionaries, reaping in joy where they had so often sowed with tears!

The tide had now turned. Opposers were

still found, but the hand of the Mighty One sent showers of blessings on most of the islands. There was a great turning unto the Lord. And the reality of their conversion was proved by the change which took place in their once wicked lives. They ceased to tell lies, to steal, to fight, to be impure, to worship idols. One chief hung his most splendid idols by the neck in their former temple. The missionary asked him:

"Why did you hang your idols in the temple?"

"I hung them there to show all the people that they be dead," was his sensible reply.

"Will you give me one of them?" said the missionary.

"Yes; they are of no use to me."

Now, do you wonder that Mr. Turner, after seeing these wonders of grace, wrote in a joyous spirit:

"I now thank God for bringing me to see his glory here. O what I have seen!

Hundreds converted from dumb idols to serve the living God."

A little later he might have written *thousands* instead of hundreds, since, in six years subsequent to the arrival of Mr. Thomas, more than eight thousand heathens had become Christians. To-day the Tonga islanders are no longer heathens, but a Christian people. Behold! what hath God wrought!

CHAPTER IX.

A LOVELY AND HEROIC LADY.

> " It is not they who idly dwell
> In cloister grey and hermit's cell,
> In prayer and vigil night and day
> Wearing all their lives away,
>   Lord of heaven, that serve thee well."

A BRIDAL party in Aberdeen, Scotland, a few hours after the marriage ceremony, was notified that the hour had arrived for the bride and bridegroom to leave the home of the bride's mother. The bride was a lovely, cultivated lady of twenty-three. Though in good health, she had found herself scarcely able to stand during the marriage service; and now that she was summoned to quit the house of her youth, she clung to her weeping mother's embraces with such an unrelaxing grasp that she was literally torn from her arms and borne to the carriage at the door.

What did this violent grief import? Was she an unwilling bride? By no means. She had married the man she had long loved. Wherefore, then, was she apparently so loth to go with him to her destined home? Strange as it may appear to you, she was more than willing, she was even glad, to go with her husband, but she was overcome by the depth of her affection for her mother, to whom she felt that she was bidding a final and earthly farewell.

But why was that parting likely to be final? Simply for the reason that the man she had married was about to take her with him across the almost unmeasurable seas to the Friendly Islands, whither he was going as a Wesleyan missionary. She had joyfully consented to become this young missionary's bride. Her mother had smiled upon her purpose to go to those heathen isles, saying, though with streaming eyes, "Go; and may the Almighty go with you." Yet when the dreaded parting moment came, their mutual affection almost forbade what their consciences, their wills, their devotion to

Christ moved them to do. The struggle was severe; but it was a voluntary sacrifice. After they were parted the bride's heroic devotion to the Christ she loved, and her desire to win the heathen of those distant Pacific Islands to his service, calmed her feelings and enabled her to face the discomforts and perils of the long tedious voyage with cheerfulness and hope.

This heroic lady's name was now MARGARET CARGILL. She and her husband sailed from England in October, 1832. After some detention in New South Wales, through her illness, they reached their appointed field of labor in Tonga, in January, 1834. Other Wesleyan missionaries had been there for several years. They found the good seed springing up beautifully in most of those lovely isles, and the native converts greeted their arrival with words of love and deeds of kindness. Said one, "It is well you have sailed toward this place," and his words expressed the welcome given them by many others.

With happy hearts this devoted pair entered

with affectionate zeal on the work before them, which, however, was not without its trials, hardships, and dangers. Mr. Cargill had to make perilous trips from one island to another in frail canoes, over seas which were often rough. The natives were not all Christians, and some of them were at times troublesome. Yet so mightily did the Holy Spirit work with the word preached, that our missionaries and their associates joyfully reaped a rich harvest of souls. They soon witnessed the conversion of hundreds, most of whom could say, as one did in a love-feast: "I am very happy to-day. My mind is full of the love of the Lord. I love him because of his love to me in pardoning my sins;" or, as another of these converts said, "The Spirit of the Lord operates within me like fire, and my mind is thereby warm." Such confessions of faith heard amid revival scenes which were like Pentecost in power, were esteemed a rich reward for all their discomforts by this truly noble and devoted pair.

But scarcely a year had passed before their

missionary zeal and Church loyalty were put to a very severe test. The "District Meeting," held at the close of the year, appointed Mr. Cargill and a colleague, named Cross, to open a mission in Fiji. This was, indeed, a call to do heroic work. The Fijians were still savages, cannibals, warriors, as debased a people as could be found in any of the Polynesian islands. Not many weeks had passed since our missionaries had been told the particulars of a horrid feast at which two hundred men and one hundred women were slaughtered, cooked, and eaten in one of the Fiji Islands! They knew that many white men had been killed and eaten by those barbarians, that women and children were quite commonly murdered and eaten as delicacies by the cruel chieftains of those islands, so beautiful in their landscapes, so rich in fruits and flowers, yet inhabited by some three hundred thousand of the vilest specimens of the human race. They had been given to expect that Tonga was to be their field of labor for many years. Yet unexpectedly, suddenly, without previous intimations, the authorities of the mission had said to them, "You must go to Fiji!" No doubt this appointment was a compliment to Mr. Cargill's ability. It expressed the estimation in which his power to do missionary work was held by the District Meeting. Nevertheless it was a sore test of their loyalty.

How did the delicate and graceful Mrs. Cargill receive it? No doubt it startled her, disappointed her, awakened her womanly fears. But her meek reply to her husband when he told her of it is worthy to be written in letters of gold. Without one resentful word she said:

"Well, David, I did not expect it to be so; but the Lord knows what is good for us. If it be his will that we should go to Fiji, I am content."

O faithful wife! O trusting believer! O heroic soul! She saw God's providence in the action of the Church authorities; she submitted to his will; she was content to suffer in Fiji if he required it. She was a Christian heroine of the noblest order.

The day of Mr. and Mrs. Cargill's departure from Tonga was one of grief to the people with whom they had labored so lovingly and successfully. In great numbers they gathered on the shore to bid them farewell. They wept, they rent the air with loud cries of sorrow. The general feeling was voiced by many who said,

"We shall never forget your love to us, nor shall we cease to love and pray for you."

It was hard for this brave little missionary band, consisting of Messrs. Cargill and Cross, with their families, to sail away from such affectionate souls, and to look forward to their meeting with the savages of Fiji, who were more likely to kill than to receive them kindly. But they trusted in God, as the stripling David did when he went forth to contend with the gigantic Goliath. In due time the little schooner which bore them approached the island of Lakemba; but her captain dared not run her inside the reefs which surrounded it until he knew whether the Fijians would treat him and these missionaries as foes or friends. To settle this question Mr. Cargill and his colleague, Mr. Cross, heroically said,

"Send us ashore in your boat. We will go and see the island chief."

The boat was lowered. The two brave missionaries stepped on board. With no little peril the boat's crew rowed her through a surf-beaten channel in the reef. As she neared the beach, some two hundred natives, mostly men armed with muskets, spears, clubs, bows and arrows, stood on the shore. They were nearly nude. Their faces were painted, some with jet black, others with red. They gazed with silent astonishment at their visitors, but made no sign either of violence or fear. It required even a loftier courage for two unarmed men to land in face of such grim warriors than for a troop of trained soldiers to mount a breach. But these good men's souls were filled with the courage of a lofty faith. They went calmly ashore with a native Fijian, whom they had brought with them from the Friendly Islands to act as their interpreter. Speaking first in their own tongue, they said to those barbarians:

"We are friends. We love you."

Those frowning cannibals made no reply; but very soon one of their number said through their interpreter:

"The king is waiting in a house near by. He wants to know who you are and what you want."

"We wish to see him," the missionaries replied.

On receiving this message the king went into his fortified house. The missionaries were conducted into his presence. They found him to be a very fat man six feet high. They explained the object of their visit, and were greatly encouraged when the natives, who crowded the audience-room of this barbarian king, clapped their hands with one accord as the sign of welcome to the missionaries. The chief was equally friendly. He asked many questions, and finally said:

"I will give you land. I will build you

houses. I will protect you. I will listen to your instructions."

This was a welcome more cordial then they had dared to expect. Their hearts leaped with gratitude to the God of missionaries. They hastened back to their vessel outside the reef to carry the good news to their wives and friends who were waiting with an anxiety that can be imagined but not described.

That same afternoon these noble men, with their brave wives and confiding children, landed, and were permitted, at their own request, to use the royal canoe-house on the beach as their lodging. The large canoe it sheltered they used for a bedstead, spreading mattresses on its deck.

The lynx-eyed natives watched them through every opening while daylight lasted. When darkness shut them in they tried to sleep; but myriads of mosquitoes made their first night in Fiji one of restlessness and suffering. Nevertheless, they were comforted by the hope that they should be their Master's instruments for transforming the cannibals around them into his pure, peace-loving disciples.

Finding that many of the natives could understand the Tonguese language, which these missionaries had already acquired, they were able to preach to such at once, and while they were learning that Fijian dialect, Mrs. Cargill soon interested many of the women and children of Lakemba in the words of Christ. They speedily learned to love her; and such was her sweetness of speech and manner that all the natives who became acquainted with her soon fell into the habit of saying, when any one spoke of her,

"Mrs. Cargill is a lady of a loving spirit."

Their first converts were won within a month after landing. They were not Fijians, however, but people from Tonga living among them, and who had been taught the Gospel by Wesleyan missionaries in their native isles. Yet their conversion led the people of Lakemba, especially their chief, to think seriously of the Gospel. But when a very destructive hurricane swept over the island, they were at first inclined to believe their priests, who said:

"The god of Lakemba is angry because the missionaries are allowed to teach on his island. He has, therefore, called all the gods of Fiji to help him. They mean to send ten storms to punish you."

But the king replied: "If the missionaries be the object of the god's anger, why does he punish us who have not left his service?"

Finding the priest made no response to this shrewd question, the chief grew bolder, and said:

"Tuilakemba is either a lying or a foolish god."

This sprightly chief was right. The god of his long-deluded people was both false and foolish, and his power was about to be taken away from him. In about five years after Messrs. Cargill and Cross began their labors in Lakemba there were over five hundred converts in the Wesleyan societies among the Fiji Islands. Besides these, there was not less than a thousand

A Lovely and Heroic Lady.

who had ceased to be heathens. These were not all won to the truth by those first missionaries, since others had been sent to aid them. But they were the first seed-sowers in those terrible cannibal islands. To-day there are more than a hundred thousand souls in Fiji who bow the knee with grateful love before the cross of Jesus, their beloved Lord. Both idolatry and cannibalism have fallen before the Gospel of love.

But the heroine of this sketch was only permitted to see the first-fruits of this truly wonderful harvest. On June 2, 1840, when only thirty-one years of age, she slept the sleep of the just in the island of Rewa, Fiji.

She loved life not so much for its own sake as because she loved the people of those sin-cursed islands. To her children and her husband she was bound by the ties of a love as pure and strong as ever swelled the heart of woman. Yet when Death came, she met him with the same submissive courage as she had always shown in obeying the voices of duty. Seeing her husband weep, she said:

"Come near me, David, that I may bless you before I die." He approached her. She threw her arms about his neck, kissed him, and added, "May my love be with you, and may the love of God fill you now and forever?"

When her end was near her husband asked, "Are you really going to leave me, Margaret?"

"Jesus bids me come," was her sweet response, and, filled with joy, she did her Lord's bidding.

One of the Fijian chiefs, when viewing her dead body, said: "She is like herself, and appears to be asleep. There lies a lady who was never angry with us, and who always smiled when we entered her house."

This, from a man who was not a Christian, but often a persecutor, was an expressive compliment to the sweet gentleness, the womanly heroism, of this devoted missionary. But she heard it not, for she was gone to the audience-chamber of the King of kings, to be greeted with his smile, and crowned with the beauty of the life eternal.

CHAPTER X.

GOING TO "CEYLON'S ISLE."

"Still shines the light of holy lives
   Like star beams over doubt;
Each sainted memory, Christ-like, drives
   Some dark possession out."—WHITTIER.

DR. THOMAS COKE is not unfitly called "the father of Wesleyan foreign missions." He richly merited this most honorable title. It was he who kindled that glorious devotion to mission work by which our British Methodism has achieved its brilliant deeds for the Christ in every quarter of the globe. But it was the spirit of Christ who gave Coke the inspiration— the true missionary spirit—by which he stirred the hearts of his brethren.

That you may gain a faint idea of that spiritlisten to a remark he made one day while travel, ing in a coach with a young missionary named Clough, who was about to sail with him to Ceylon and India. During a lull in their conversation the missionary handed him a paper containing some matter of public interest. Coke, perceiving at a glance that it did not relate to their proposed work, returned it with this memorable confession:

"I beg your pardon, but excuse me; *I am dead to all things but Asia.*"

The men who lift the world out of darkness into light all have this spirit. To them, as with this missionary doctor, the work they are about to undertake is the principal object of thought, conversation, action, and desire. It possesses them.

John Wesley had talked with Dr. Coke about a mission to Asia thirty years before the latter made that memorable remark. The spark kindled by that conversation had never died out of the doctor's great heart. Busy as he was with missionary cares in the West Indies and in North America, he cherished the hope of planting Methodism in Asia, and improved every opportunity to gather information about its millions of blinded inhabitants until, in 1813, the hour for action arrived. He pleaded with the British Conference, weeping while he spoke; he pledged the money needed to start a mission in Ceylon; he proposed to begin the work in person; he succeeded in securing six men to accompany him; and was filled with a joy almost seraphic when, in December, 1813, he met all his fellow-laborers around a supper-table in Portsmouth, England, where they had assembled for the purpose of taking ship. Rising from his chair, he joyously exclaimed:

"Here we all are before God; six missionaries and two dear sisters, now embarked in the most important and glorious work in the world! Glory be to his blessed name, that he has given you to be my companions and assistants in carrying the Gospel to the poor Asiatics!"

The well-spring of this unselfish exultation was the love of Christ, filling his heart and overflowing in self-sacrificing love for miserable souls who were to be made happy by that same heavenly love. The missionary spirit is LOVE.

This band of genuine crusaders sailed from Portsmouth in two vessels, neither having sufficient comfortable accommodations for all. The first part of their voyage was auspicious; but when the ships neared the equator, Mrs. Ault, wife of one of the missionaries, passed into the bright world of the glorified. Her death made them sad. Three others of this devoted band suffered from severe sickness; but on the morning of the third of May they were all overwhelmed by a catastrophe. Doctor Coke was found by his servant, early that morning, lying dead on his cabin floor! His right cheek bore the stain of blood which had flowed from his mouth; his head was slightly turned to one side, but a placid smile rested on his countenance. The ship's surgeon judged that he must have arisen early in the night, either to call a servant or get something from the locker, and that, while crossing the cabin floor, a stroke of apoplexy deprived him of life in an instant. His work was done, and that sudden stroke was the swift but gentle messenger by which his

Lord sent to call him from the work he loved on earth to engage in still nobler service in the kingdom eternal.

To the little missionary band of which he was the chief his sudden departure was a stunning blow. He was their official leader; they had leaned upon him as their father in the work that lay before them. His great reputation, his high character, his practical wisdom, his long experience, his official relations to their Conference, his personal influence, and his pecuniary resources, had operated as antidotes to every fear of failure in Ceylon and India which had arisen in their hearts when they looked on the human side of their vocation. With such a guide and God's blessing, there could be, they had thought, no chance of failure. But his death had broken their human stay and staff. It had even beggared them, for they were poor men and their dead chief was their treasurer. His sudden death had given him no opportunity to convey to them a legal right to use the money which he had provided for their use from his own funds. The prospect of entering a strange land without money or friends was indeed dark. You cannot wonder, therefore, that when the party came together from both ships, which had not parted company, and joined in the ceremony which preceded the burial of his body in the great wide sea, they, like children bereaved of a beloved father, trembled with apprehension respecting the future. But they had faith in God; trusting in him their hearts soon found consolation, hope, and courage. O, the blessedness of faith in God!

Twenty weeks after leaving England these six missionaries, and the wife of one of them, landed in Bombay, India. So poor were they that they had not cash enough to pay for a single meal! What a trial of faith! But the God of missions had not forgotten these noble souls who were seeking to do his work. He had put it into the heart of Captain Birch, commander of the ship in which Dr. Coke died, to help them. That Christian sailor told their singular story to a Christian merchant named

Money, to whose address a letter was found among Dr. Coke's papers. And when one of the missionaries, named Harvard, called on him, with anxious heart and a clouded countenance, this noble merchant hastened to comfort him, by saying:

"I am acquainted with your situation. I shall be very happy to advance you money on the credit of your society at home."

Thus did the light from their glorified Master's face break forth upon them through the dark cloud which had risen from the mysterious removal of their trusted leader. Nor was this merchant the only friend He gave them in Bombay. Sir Evan Nepean, Governor of Bombay, who, when a boy, had heard Wesley preach, gave them the use of his own house during their stay. Some American missionaries visited them. The sympathies of many gentlemen were drawn toward them. After all their painful anxieties they suffered no actual want, and in due time were enabled to obtain a passage to Ceylon, Mr. Harvard remaining in Bombay on account of his wife, who was too feeble at that time to take another voyage.

Letters from the friendly merchant and from Governor Nepean to Lord Molesworth, commander of the British forces at Galle, Ceylon, had prepared that gentleman and his most excellent lady to give our missionaries a very cordial reception. Being disciples of Jesus, with large, liberal views, this noble pair did every thing in their power to help them begin their Christian work. Not the least of his favors was his offer to give them the superintendence of the public schools, with salaries, at the stations they might choose to occupy. This offer they gladly accepted, and, after selecting suitable points, they separated and entered on their work at Jaffna, Matura, and Batticaloa. One of their number, Mr. Clough, remaining to do mission work at Galle.

If the sudden death of their great leader had tempted these sorely tried men to doubt God's approval of their work, their reception in Ceylon speedily dissolved that temptation. At every place they were greeted most cordially, not only by officers of government, but also by foreign and native merchants, and by religious men among the soldiers. Episcopalians, Baptists, and even Catholics, wished them Godspeed. Ceylon became to them a field ripe for the harvest. Hence, with genuine Methodistic zeal, they began teaching the young, preaching to English-speaking people, of whom they found many, studying the native languages, and, after a brief space, preaching to the natives through interpreters, and finally in their own tongues.

A few months after their arrival Mr. Clough became God's instrument in bringing a learned and distinguished Buddhist priest to the knowledge of his Son. His name was Petrus Panditti Sekara. He was a preacher of the faith of his ancestors. But, while studying that faith, his heart rebelled against it, because, as he said, he "found in that religion no Redeemer to save our souls from death, no Creator of the world, or a beginning to it." While troubled about this lack in his creed, he met with our missionary, Clough. This gentleman talked with him about Jesus, and gave him a copy of the Gospels in the Singalese tongue. After much reading of these sacred books, and many conversations with Mr. Clough, this determined man said:

"I will abjure the religion of Buddha; I will embrace the religion of Christ!"

His fellow-priests, hearing of his purpose, made great efforts to persuade him to change his purpose. Fifty-seven head priests reasoned with him. "You will ruin our religion in this country if *you* forsake the priesthood," said they. His family also entreated him, with tears, not to disgrace them. Some of them said, "We will kill ourselves if you do." His life was threatened, and he was forced to flee from his temple to escape death. But the heroic man stood firm, as a deeply-rooted rock. To become a Christian was to forfeit office, property, and old friends; nevertheless, he had the courage to request Mr. Clough to baptize him. A day or two before this beautiful rite was administered he said to his spiritual father:

"I dreamed last night that my robes were covered with all kinds of filthy reptiles. I was so disgusted that I went to a river and cast them in, never to touch them again. When I awoke this morning I found my robes folded up and thrown on the far side of the room. Now, thought I, God has sent me this dream to show me the bad state I am in, and to confirm me in all my former resolutions. I am only sorry that I am forced to put the robes on again."

A few days later he threw away his yellow priestly robes, and professed himself a disciple of Christ by being publicly baptized. He supposed he was forsaking all by that act. But God provided for him through the governor, who appointed him translator to the government, with a fixed salary. His conversion shook the faith of many in Buddhism, and prepared the way for that remarkable success which afterward crowned the labors of the Wesleyan missionaries.

The climate of Ceylon, with steady and hard work, brought debility and sickness to several of those heroic men. To Mr. Ault it brought death. His trip from Galle to Batticaloa was made by water in a wretched barge. During the rough passage he was much exposed and narrowly escaped a watery grave. His grief on account of the death of his beloved wife on the voyage from England still preyed on his spirits. His zeal in his work completed what grief and exposure had begun. On the first of April, 1815, with no European near him, he asked his Malabar servant to read him a chapter from Holy Scripture. The man obeyed. When he finished Mr. Ault made a few brief remarks upon it, turned in his bed, and quietly passed from the field of his missionary labors to the throne of the Lord of missions. His missionary life was short, but it left a lasting impression of the beauty of a Christian life on the minds of the people who witnessed his purity and loving zeal.

Our missionaries were not content with preaching and teaching only, but sought every opportunity to converse with the natives about

Jesus. Among their visitors at Colombo, for such conversation, was a priest known as the *Ava Priest*. This man drove a splendid equipage. In appearance he was very dignified. In mind he was acute and thoughtful. In scholarship he was learned, not only in the writings of his religion, but also in general literature and science. The natives were proud of his reputation, and very highly respected his character.

This man met Messrs. Clough and Harvard every day for several weeks, disputing against their doctrines. At first he was very bitter against the truth. After some time a change passed over his spirit. Silenced in argument he listened to the truth with the docility of a little child. Then the Holy Spirit convinced him of sin, and he began to pray, first for wisdom, then for mercy. To prove his sincerity he permitted Mr. Harvard to preach Jesus at the door of a Buddhist temple, in front of a great idol, to a large assembly of priests and people. The text of the sermon was, "We know that an idol is nothing in the world, and that there is none other God but one."

This Ava Priest became a converted man, was publicly baptized by the name of George Nadoris de Silva, became an eloquent preacher of the truth, and did eminent service against the false religion in which he had been trained.

Methodism soon grew into strength in Ceylon. Hundreds of the heathen natives were converted; thousands of heathen children were taught the truth which set them free from the chains of their ancient religion; and vast numbers of the nominal Christians found by our missionaries in Ceylon were led to exchange their dead faith for a living trust in Him, who, though once crucified, now liveth for evermore. Thus did this misssion, so imperiled at first by the sudden death of Dr. Coke, become a thing of power. Perhaps Coke's mysterious death so drew out the powers of these six young men who leaned upon him, that they accomplished vastly more than if he had lived to think and plan and act in their behalf. Who knows?

CHAPTER XI.

THE GRAVE-YARD OF MISSIONARIES.

"Each one performs his life-work and then leaves it:
Those that come after him will estimate
His influence on the age in which he lived."
—LONGFELLOW.

THE Dark Continent named Africa has, on its western coast, a colony called Sierra Leone, which owes it origin to a settlement of colored men who joined the British army during our Revolutionary War, and were taken to England with that army when our flag triumphed. Granville Sharp, Wilberforce, and other good men sent these poor freedmen to Sierra Leone. Other poor creatures, wrested from slave-ships by the English navy, were afterward settled there. So that it has grown to be a region of considerable importance to African commerce, and has quite a large population.

Some of those settlers had heard the Gospel

from the lips of Methodist preachers in America. They kept it in their hearts as a precious treasure, and it kept them from sinking back into the heathenism of their ancestors. In 1808 these faithful souls wrote to Dr. Adam Clarke for a Wesleyan missionary, and Dr. Coke, who delighted in mission work, after some delay, which made his great heart bleed, found a noble brother named GEORGE WARREN, who was not only willing but desirous to go, and to preach Jesus in that land of almost certain death to natives of Europe.

George Warren, like Timothy of Holy Writ, had been taught to love the Scriptures when a child. Christ, dwelling in his heart, had given him a burning desire to tell the old, old story to the dark sons of Africa. But when he told Dr. Coke he was ready to go, his parents fearing he might fall a victim to fever, objected. Then this devoted man wrote them, saying,

"I beseech you by the blood of souls not to hinder me from going!"

His earnestness conquered his father, who

withdrew his objections. His mother died soon after. Then he left his comfortable station in Cornwall, and sailed to Sierra Leone in 1811. When the pious little band, who had waited for a missionary, saw him land, they were filled with rapture, exclaiming,

"This is what we have been praying for so long, and now the Lord has answered our prayers!"

Hundreds flocked to his preaching-place. He soon saw his work bear fruit. His heart was glad. He looked forward hopefully when, to the grief of his loving flock, the pitiless fever struck him, and he died only a little more than eight months after his arrival. He soon won the missionary's crown in glory.

"A missionary wanted for Sierra Leone." Two years passed before this note in the Wesleyan Minutes met with a response. The death of the noble Warren had chilled the zeal of many. At last, Mr. William Davies and his accomplished wife replied, "We will go!" They went, and their labors soon made the people glad. Mrs. Davies gathered a school of one hundred and fifty girls. The wilderness began to blossom when, alas! ten months had scarcely passed before this heroic couple were both smitten with fever on the same day. A few days of suffering followed, and then the purified soul of the missionary's wife ascended to the throne of her glorified Lord. The people placed a tombstone on her grave, with this fitting inscription, "NOT LOST, BUT GONE BEFORE!"

The bereaved husband recovered. Not long after he had resumed his labors he was praying for a poor, penitent native in the prayer-room, when a cry of joy was heard in a distant corner. The next moment the missionary found himself in the arms of the penitent, who was crying, "I found him! I found him!"

"What have you found?" inquired Mr. Davies, who was still firmly embraced in the man's arms.

"I found Christ. I feel his pardoning peace. His Spirit says, 'Go in peace; thy sins are forgiven thee,'" replied the man, no longer a weeping penitent, but a rejoicing believer in the Lamb of God.

This scene, odd though it was, comforted the afflicted missionary's heart. Still greater was his consolation when, after preaching a few times in one of the outlying village, he saw the head-man of the place bring a bag filled with *greegrees* into an open space. These *greegrees* were bits of leather, horn, or paper, on which the priests had written some Arabic words, which were supposed to give them power to keep those who bought them from harm. "Bring shavings, sticks, and straw!" said the man with the bag to the people. His command was obeyed, and then, emptying the contents of his bag upon the burning sticks, he let the fire consume all those pretended amulets.

The people gazed on this strange spectacle. Wonder, mingled with fear, kept them silent. Presently one man spoke in a melancholy tone, saying,

"What me do now for *greegree* to keep me?"

To him an old man replied, sharply, "Hold your tongue, you! We tink *greegree* keep we from the big fire, and he no can keep himself from burning before my eye. Me be fool no longer. Me seek white men God; me seek Massa Jesus to save me."

To win these simple people to Christ was meat and drink to this devoted missionary. He rejoiced to see the good work spread, and wrote home, saying, "I need help." Mr. Samuel Brown and his faithful wife offered themselves as reapers in this dangerous field, and were sent out to join him in 1816. They began work with bright hopes of success, when, alas! only seven months after their arrival, the fever smote them, and Mrs. Brown died, and was buried in the same grave with the lamented Mrs. Davies.

Mr. Brown recovered, and resumed his labors with marked success, though Mr. Davies, owing to repeated attacks of fever, was obliged to return to England. But Christ was with him, and helped him turn many to righteousness. Yet such was the deadly nature of the climate that Mr. Brown's removal became necessary in 1819. But who would be willing to succeed him? Three had died in the work in the short space of less than seven years. Were there any more heroic souls ready to die for poor African sinners? Of course there were, for the love that brought Jesus from his throne in heaven to die on the cross never fails to move some of his disciples to put their lives in peril whenever his work requires such a sacrifice.

The two heroes who went to take Brown's place were single men, named John Baker and John Gillison. They found more than two hundred and fifty souls serving the Saviour. They soon saw several who had been makers of *gree-grees* turn unto the Lord. Their prospering work made them very happy when, for the fourth time, death demanded another noble victim. Six months after his arrival, John Gillison fell beneath the deadly fever's sudden stroke. He was only twenty-two years old when he left his earthly habitation to go and take possession of the mansion not made with hands. Yet his life was not short, if, as a poet says,

"That life is *long* which answers life's great end."

John Baker, in spite of weakness caused by repeated attacks of fever, kept the field, fighting death with one hand and Satan with the other. He was mighty against both, and by 1821 had no less than seven hundred and forty rejoicing souls under his pastoral care. The story of his success had moved others to venture their lives, and in that year he had the pleasure of greeting Mr. and Mrs. Huddlestone and Mr. Lane as fellow-laborers in that land so fatal to the lives of missionaries. For himself he chose not to return to England, but to go to the river Gambia, and begin new work in a region thought to be less sickly than Sierra Leone. He was to be aided in this latter work by Mr. Morgan, another noble volunteer in this perilous portion of the Lord's great harvest-field.

Messrs. Baker and Morgan suffered many hardships on the banks of the Gambia, but were not long without evidence that God's truth could work wonders in the hearts of the depraved natives. Their first convert was a poor woman at a village called St. Mary's. "O massa, my heart trouble me too much," was her confession after hearing them preach a few times. They told her of the sinner's Friend. She soon after met in class, where she said to Mr. Morgan,

"Me went into the bush, and put me knee down on the ground, and me pray, and pray, till all my trouble go away. Me glad too much, and me praise my Massa Jesus; and then me pray for my poor husband that my Massa Jesus would save him."

These very simple words are beautiful because of their simplicity. And although their speaker was an untaught black woman, they decribe the manner in which souls are saved through penitence and faith in Jesus as clearly as it could be done by any white Christian scholar. Is it any wonder that our missionaries felt their hearts grow warm toward such converts; or that, as fast as one of them died at his post, other heroic spirits in the Wesleyan Church stood ready to step in and fill the gaps made by the remorseless hand of Death?

It seemed at times as if Satan, eager to take revenge for their success against his kingdom, was goading Death to destroy the missionaries by whom it was achieved. In the two years preceding 1830 no less than four Wesleyan missionaries and one missionary's wife died in that West African work. In less than forty years from the opening of the mission, over fifty-four missionary laborers laid down their lives in that land of many European graves.

Fifty-four heroes in about forty years dying, not for fame or riches or earthly honors, but for the privilege of telling poor, ignorant, degraded men, women, and children about Jesus and his love! What a glorious page this sad fact makes in the history of Methodism! Surely nothing but the Spirit of Christ could have made so many persons willing to step into the places of those who first fell at their posts. Remember, they were not *persuaded* to do it by their friends. They were *volunteers* in the fullest sense of that word. One of those morally grand men, named William Rowland Peck, in telling how he came to go, said, of a great missionary meeting at which he was present when only nineteen years old, "Such times as these fill me with zeal for the conversion of sinners. O, my soul yearns over them! O, that I might go and tell them Jesus died! O, how I long to be traversing the weary plains of Africa! The more I hear of the dangers and difficulties of a missionary life in Africa the more anxious I am to go."

This was the spirit which moved Mr. Peck— the true missionary spirit breathed into his soul by Him who died for sinners. Had it been the mere enthusiasm of an excited lad, it would have died, like the brightness of a pleasing dream. But being heaven-born, it was a sacred flame nothing earthly could put out. It burned steadily through three years, when the opportunity was given him to gratify his desire.

Then he told his mother whither he was going. Her heart swelled with anguish, and she exclaimed,

"Roland, if you go to Western Africa, you will be the death of me."

This appeal of mother-love to his affection for her was a painful test of his love to Christ. But, though he loved her dearly, he loved Jesus still more. Hence, with tears in his eyes, he tenderly replied,

"Mother, if you do not consent to my going to Africa, you will be the death of *me!*"

Thus did his love for Jesus prove itself stronger than his love for his mother. And she, good, devoted soul, after much prayer, consented to his going, saying,

"I see it is of the Lord, and I will not resist his will."

Nor did she, but went with his fond father to see him ordained. On that solemn occasion she heard him say, in burning words, "I am not only willing to go to Africa, but I long to go!"

And he went, was received gladly by the people, was very successful in saving souls, and alas! after about six months, was laid low by the pitiless coast fever. Was he sorry, think you, when tossing with fever and racked with the pains of death, that he had given himself up to missionary work in Africa? Not in the least degree. It was not of his own death that he thought, but of what he feared might be its effect on the friends of missions at home.

"Nothing," said he, the day before his death, "nothing grieves me so much as the thought that my death will cause the hands of our friends in England to hang down."

"O, unselfish soul! No wonder that in his last moment he tried to sing,

> "Happy, if with my latest breath
> I may but gasp His name;"

or that, when his voice sank into silence, he lifted his hands to heaven in token of the victory which was even then crowning his freed soul as it ascended from the pestiferous atmosphere of Africa into the house of the glorified.

It was because the self-denying spirit of this noble missionary lived in the Wesleyan Church that it never lacked volunteers eager to go to that grave-yard of missionaries, Western Africa.

CHAPTER XII.

IN THE LAND OF THE NAMAQUAS.

"With weary hand, yet steadfast wills,
   In old age as in youth
The Master found thee sowing still
   The good seed of his truth."—WHITTIER.

NEARLY seventy years ago a Wesleyan minister, about twenty-seven years of age, informed the Wesleyan Conference that he desired to go into the foreign missionary work. Knowing him to be a man of energy, as well as of ability, the Conference accepted his offer, and the Missionary Committee bade him go to Ceylon. Cheerfully accepting this important and prosperous work, BARNABAS SHAW, with his pious wife, immediately began his preparations for the long voyage to that distant isle.

But, as in an army, soldiers often have to be ordered from one post to another, so it at times became necessary for the Wesleyan Missionary

Committee to change the appointment of their missionaries. Hence, while Mr. Shaw was in London getting ready for Ceylon, he was requested to go to South Africa instead. The Wesleyan Mission to the latter country had previously failed, owing to the opposition of the colonial government. It was thought that the time had now come to make another attempt. Mr. Shaw seemed to be the right man to do this. He knew it was a more difficult field than Ceylon, that he would have to battle with many difficulties without a colleague—at least for a season. Nevertheless, having a heroic soul, burning with desire to carry the good news of salvation to the heathen of any land, he cheerfully consented, and sailed in December, 1815, for the Cape of Good Hope. After a stormy voyage, during which he and his wife had to witness the burial of their infant daughter, in mid-ocean, he landed in Cape Town, and, as soon as convenient, waited on Lord Somerset, the governor of the colony, to ask permission to open his mission in that place.

His papers were of the highest character. The governor could not object to them. Yet, though very courteous in speech, he very decidedly refused to give the desired permission. "There are plenty of clergymen here," said he, "for all the English and Dutch; and the slaveholders are unwilling to have missionaries preach to the colored people."

This coldly polite speech was to Barnabas Shaw what a chilling fog is to a landscape. But the warmth of his love for souls, and his strong native courage, soon revived his spirits. "If the governor," he thought, "is afraid of the Dutch and English preachers and of the slaveholders, I need not fear them. I ought to obey God rather than men. And I will."

This noble thought had life in it. It moved him to make inquiries among the English soldiers stationed at Cape Town. He soon found that a few pious souls among them were in the habit of meeting for prayer in a room hired by them for that purpose. To them, therefore, Mr. Shaw preached, the Sunday after his arrival, "the first Methodist sermon ever heard in South Africa."

Encouraged by this opening, Mr. Shaw visited two other military stations, within twenty miles of Cape Town, where, also, he met with a cordial welcome from little bands of men who were both soldiers of England and of the kingdom of Christ. These devout warriors hung with delight on his fervent lips. He did them good, no doubt, but his soul yearned for access to the unnumbered Hottentots, Kaffirs, Negroes, and others, scattered over the vast territory, two thousand miles long by two thousand miles broad, which lay between Cape Town and the Equator, and was known to the world as South Africa.

How can I reach those untaught souls? was the question which burned itself into his heart. The God of missions soon answered it by bringing into Cape Town a missionary with a dozen converted heathen from the land of the Namaquas. This good man's name was Schmelen. He was employed by the London Missionary Society, but, in the liberal spirit of a true missionary, he urged Mr. Shaw to return with him, and start a Wesleyan mission among some of the Namaqua tribes.

The sight of those converted Namaquas, the persuasions of the devoted Schmelen, the cheerful consent of Mrs. Shaw to accompany him, and the prospect of a promising field, determined Mr. Shaw to attempt the long, tedious journey into the country of the Namaquas. Suppose you join them on their way thither, it will give you a faint idea of what missionaries have often endured when seeking to preach Jesus to the heathen in their homes of poverty and woe.

Their vehicle is not a trimly painted stagecoach, drawn by a spirited team of horses, but a large four-wheeled wagon covered with canvas, and drawn by a team of sixteen or eighteen oxen. If you will peep at its interior, you will see that it is fitted up with chests. One of these in front and another behind are for crockeryware, for bread, tea, sugar, and other small articles. Along its sides are boxes for hammers, axes, and other tools. Its floor is mostly covered with trunks and bags filled with clothing and other useful things for a missionary station in a lone land. Over the chests and packages in the rear there is a frame-work for a mattress on which the travelers expect to sleep. The little space left in the front part of the wagon is to be used as a sitting-room. It is a clumsy, cumberous concern, without springs, but it is to be the house of our brave missionary and his heroic wife for weeks, while they journey along the wretched trails toward the lost people whom they seek to save.

You can form a picture in your mind of Mr. Shaw and his wife seated in this bungling machine. One Hottentot, armed with a very long whip, is on the driver's seat; another is in front of the long ox-team to guide the oxen; one or two others follow behind, driving a small flock of sheep to be used for food on the long journey. These Hottentots are also expected to help in preparing the nightly encampments and in cooking food.

On the 6th of September, 1816, our missionaries quit Cape Town. A few pious soldiers and other friends go with them to their first halting-place, where, after prayer, they bid them farewell. The missionary party, which includes the faithful Schemlen and his converted Namaquas, moves on until late in the evening, when it halts for the night. Not having the inside of their wagon properly stowed, Mr. and Mrs. Shaw cannot use their mattress, but have to sleep as best they can, reclining among their boxes and bags. Depend upon it, their sleep that night was broken and unrestful.

The first person Mr. Shaw saw, when he crept out of his comfortless lodging the next morning, was his friend Schmelen, sitting under a bush, stirring his cup of coffee with a dry twig. A happy smile lighted his kindly face, while he said, "Good-morning, sir;" and then, holding up his twig, he added, "This is a Namaqua spoon."

After partaking of a rustic breakfast served with little ceremony the party gathered for worship, in which the converted natives joined very devoutly.

Proceeding on their journey, at the slow rate of some ten or twelve miles a day, for about eighteen days, they met with the usual difficulties of South African travel. Rough roads, overflowing rivers without bridges, stretches of desert in which was no water, steep, stony hills, and swampy vales impeded their progress. Yet they pressed on undismayed, cheered by the hope of finding, not gold, or silver, or diamonds, or houses, or lands, but human souls to whom they might tell "that sweet story of old" about the riches of heavenly grace.

After traveling about two hundred miles, they were surprised one day by hearing a Namaqua exclaim:

"The chief of the Little Namaquas, with four of his people, is coming!"

Our party halted. The chief approached. He told a story which made the heart of Barnabas Shaw leap for joy. He had heard, he said, of the "Great Word," and was on his way to Cape Town to find a teacher. After hearing his story, Mr. Shaw thought he saw, in this chief's presence, the finger of God pointing him to his land and tribe as a suitable field of labor. "I will go with you to your kraal," said he, to the chief, who was so delighted, on hearing these words, that he shed tears of joy and gladness.

The generous Schmelen went with Mr. Shaw to the home of this inquiring chief, two hundred miles from the place where he met them. The Namaquas gave our missionary as cordial a greeting as he could desire. Finding them willing to aid him in every way possible to them, and eager to be taught the truth, Mr. Shaw concluded to remain at Lily Fountain, as the place was named. The good Schmelen went on his way to Great Namaqualand, and Barnabas Shaw and his noble wife, left alone among a savage people, founded the first Wesleyan mission station in South Africa, at Lily Fountain.

A missionary cannot, ought not, to live as

savage people do. Hence, Mr. Shaw had to build a little cottage, fence, dig, and plant a garden, and make such furniture as tables, bedsteads, and chairs. The Namaquas helped him, but they were so unused to steady work, and so slow to learn the use of tools, that our missionary had to be in good part his own workman. But he toiled cheerfully, preached to them through an interpreter, opened a school, began to study their language, and explored the surrounding country as far as the Orange River. All this made his work very, very wearisome. At the same time he and his patient wife had to suffer many privations. But faith and hope made their hearts strong and happy.

The good seed soon began to grow among the simple-minded Namaquas. Its first shoots appeared in their efforts to live less like savages, and to form new habits of labor and life. After a time the truth led some of them to weep over their sins, and to seek Jesus. Said one of his first converts, "I believe Jesus has more love for a sinner than any mother for her child."

Another said, "When I think of the love of God in the gift of his Son, my thoughts stand still, I am dumb with silence." Only eight months after arriving at Lily Fountain, Mr. Shaw had the unspeakable pleasure of baptizing seventeen adult converts and eleven children. This was, indeed, success. And those converts proved to be true and loyal. They kept the faith, and from that time onward Jesus had a constantly increasing band of disciples, not only at Lily Fountain, but also in other parts of Namaqualand.

When this good news reached England, and Mr. Shaw reported that the people were far too many for one man to teach, the Missionary Committee, in due time, sent out other self-denying men to help this successful man. Then the work spread in many directions, and for ten years continued under the supervision of its energetic pioneer and his heroic wife.

Lions were numerous in South Africa. Our missionary was often in danger from their attack when on his missionary journeys.

Venomous snakes were also plentiful. Once, when he and his wife were encamped in the open air, that good lady, in moving the bed-covering with a view to placing their mattress in a suitable spot on which to pass the night, saw a venomous puff adder curled up beneath the bolster. But for this timely discovery it is likely that both of them would have ended their earthly lives that night.

One of Mr. Shaw's assistants, eager to preach to the tribes beyond the Orange River, started on a tour of observation, with two native exhorters for companions. Some vile Bushmen coveted the few articles they carried with them, and one night, while they were asleep, fired poisoned arrows on the two natives, and killed them. The young missionary, awakened by the noise, and seeing the fierce Bushmen at hand, rose, fled to the shelter of a bush, and kneeled down to pray. While in that act a heavy stone from a Bushman's arm struck him a mortal blow on the head. Thus he fell by a murderer's hand; but did he not ascend from that blood-stained spot to join the noble army of martyrs in the land of the redeemed? Without doubt he won a martyr's glorious crown.

In 1827 Mr. and Mrs. Shaw, with their son Barnabas—they had buried two children in the land of the Namaquas—returned to England, to rest and recruit. But his heart was in Africa, and although he still loved his native land, he returned, with his wife, early in 1829. After spending eight years in Cape Town and vicinity, his wife's health required his second return to the land of his birth. This time he spent six years preaching with success on English circuits. Then a loud cry for more help from the brethren in Namaqualand was to Mr. Shaw what the blast of a trumpet is to a veteran war-horse. Again he volunteered to go to South Africa. He was warmly greeted in Cape Town; but his declining strength rendering his going again to the land of the Namaquas unadvisable, he spent the remainder of his active years doing circuit work within the bounds of the Cape Colony. He lived until June, 1857, when, being nearly seventy years of age, he quietly passed from the land he loved, to take his appointed place before the great white throne of his beloved Master.

CHAPTER XIII.

PERILS AND TRIALS OF MISSIONARY LIFE.

> " Pour blessèd Gospel, glorious news for man!
> Thy stream of life o'er springless deserts roll,
> Thy bond of peace the mighty earth can span,
> And make one brotherhood from pole to pole."
> —C. ASHWORTH.

MODERN missionaries who go from their native land to distant countries, like Saint Paul in more ancient times, have to reckon among the dangers they must face the perils of the great, wide sea. A startling example of one such peril is given by ELIJAH HOOLE, a Wesleyan missionary, who, in 1820, was sent from England to Madras, India.

In company with Mr. James Mowat and wife, who were going to the same mission, he found himself, after a quick passage, near the end of his voyage in the ship "Tanjore." Then at the close of a fine warm day in September a thunderstorm burst forth, but caused no unusual alarm. Mr. Hoole was on deck taking a farewell view of the mountains of Ceylon, where the ship had recently landed a few passengers. A heavy cloud with a luminous center met his eye. He pointed it out to the captain, who thought it harmless. Then the storm became more and more violent, and the missionary retreated from the rushing rain to the shelter of the cuddy. Presently a terrific flash of lightning struck the ship. The roar and crackling of the thunder which accompanied it was deafening. A passenger near the cuddy door was prostrated. Two seamen fell dead on the deck.

Then the voice of the second mate was heard loudly shouting,

"Fire in the hold! Fire below!"

At that alarming cry every soul on board rushed to the deck. Pumps were manned, buckets handed round, all joined in an effort to extinguish the fire. Vain endeavor! The flames had the mastery. The ship must be abandoned.

"Get out the boats!" was the next cry. But the long boat was already on fire. The "yawl" with much difficulty was got afloat, as was the "gig" also. Mrs. Mowat and another lady were put into the yawl. The other passengers and the ship's company were crowded into both boats, which were so overloaded that they sank to very near the water's edge. In fleeing from death by fire they ran great risk of perishing by water. Most of them were only partly clothed, and the rain, still falling in torrents, literally drenched them and compelled them to keep bailing the overloaded boats to prevent them from being swamped.

In their haste they had taken but three oars. The yawl had no rudder. The ship, by this time enveloped in flames, seemed drifting toward them. Fortunately the sea was now calm and the wind quiet. By dint of skill and toil they got their boats out of danger from the burning ship. In two hours from the time when she was struck they saw her masts fall. Shortly after the greedy sea engulfed her, and those forty-two persons found themselves without food or water in deep darkness with the certainty of sinking should the wind blow or the waters swell. Nevertheless, our missionaries were calm and peaceful, for their trust was in Him for whose work's sake they had left their happy English homes.

Slowly and painfully that night wore away. Daylight enabled them to see land ahead, but, alas for their dawning hopes! a nearer approach to it showed it to be a wild, uninhabited jungle, with a coast-line bristling with rocks forever washed by foaming breakers.

This was disheartening. The sun, glaring with brightness and intolerably hot, added to their discomfort. Death by drowning or starvation seemed inevitable, until they discovered a native vessel anchored in the distance. Toward this craft they rowed, making such signals as they could invent out of their scant clothing. After five hours of toil and anxiety they reached the vessel, and not without difficulty persuaded its owners to take them all on board. Fortunately they were not very far from Trincomalee, a city of Ceylon, where there was a Wesleyan mission station. Thither they directed their course. Forty-three hours after quitting their burning ship, our missionaries found themselves safely lodged in the Wesleyan mission house, cheered by the affectionate attentions of the two mission families who were its occupants.

They had lost books, clothing, every thing but the few garments in which they had hastily clad themselves when so suddenly driven from the burning ship. Yet their perils by sea were not ended. They had to take ship again to reach Madras. A small schooner, named the "Cochin," was the only craft available. Her little cabin was given to the two ladies of the party. The gentlemen had to sleep in hammocks slung so near together that at every motion of the vessel they rubbed one against another. This was a hardship increased by the violence of the wind. The waves ran so high that they swept over the tiny bark, threatening to engulf her. Her store of food also ran short, so that hunger was added to peril. But the Lord protected his disciples, and after three days and two nights on the deep they were permitted to land safely at Madras, in Southern India. Mr. Hoole and Mr. Mowat were appointed to begin their missionary labors by founding a new mission at a place named Bangalore, situated some distance in the interior.

Like loyal soldiers of the cross, they were desirous of starting at once for their post of duty. But their missionary brethren in Madras said to them, "You have no books, no wardrobes. You had better stay here until you can get a new supply of those things so necessary to your work. You can proceed with your study of the Tamul language, which you must learn before you can preach. We will loan you our libraries for this purpose."

This was good advice, given with generous kindness. They followed it, and devoted their time to the diligent study of the language and of the people. There was a congregation of native Wesleyans in Madras. Of course Mr.

Hoole visited it. Let me tell you what he saw there.

The chapel had no pews, only a large open space with a pulpit in the rear. The people — men, women, and children — were sitting on mats spread on the floor. The men were neatly dressed in white cotton clothes; the women in red or blue cloths, some of cotton, some of silk, nine yards long, wrapped about their persons without the aid of pins or sewing. One end was drawn over the head serving as a vail. The service began with a Tamul hymn, which the people stood up to sing. After the hymn prayers were read, during which the people all kneeled with their bodies inclined forward, almost prostrate, their hands and faces resting on the ground. After prayer came the reading of the Scriptures. Then Mr. Close, the missionary, preached in English, but repeated sentence by sentence in Tamul. Mr. Hoole noticed that the peple were "wonderfully attentive." When Mr. Close asked questions, as he frequently did, their replies showed that they understood what they heard. Of course, Mr. Hoole was highly pleased with this interesting and encouraging spectacle of a Christian congregation in a heathen land.

After a few weeks' stay in Madras, the Wesleyan missionary at Negapatam, one hundred and eighty miles south of Madras, sent for some one to help him. As it was the rainy season, and therefore unfit for Mrs. Mowat to make such a journey, Mr. Hoole consented to undertake it.

There was no railroad, no stage, no carriage to convey him to the field of his labors, nothing but horses, or a *palankeen*, which was a sort of covered cot carried on men's shoulders by means of two poles. To travel on horseback required tents for rest and sleep; it also exposed the rider to dews by night and sun-stroke by day, both very dangerous to persons unused to the climate. When Mr. Hoole saw his palankeen with its ten bearers, and six men to carry baggage and cooking utensils, he shrank from seeing human beings employed as beasts of burden. But he had to submit to the law of necessity, and crept into his palankeen, which was a double one, made to carry two persons sitting one at each end, facing each other. Being alone, he could sit or lie at full length as his comfort might require.

At four o'clock one afternoon four of the bearers took up his palankeen and started at the rate of about five miles an hour. The other bearers and the baggage carriers ran before and behind, talking, laughing, and singing. After ten minutes the bearers stopped. Four others took their places, and the march was resumed as before. This change was kept up until they reached a *choultry*, or resting-place. As there were no inns for travelers, brick or stone buildings, called choultries, which were merely four walls with a sheltering roof, stood on the highways for their free use. In one of these structures Mr. Hoole rested. A servant, hired for that purpose, prepared tea for him by lighting a fire outside the choultry, after drinking which our missionary wrapped his outer garment about him and went to sleep. At three o'clock in the morning he resumed his journey. In India, travelers journey during the greater part of the night, and sleep during the heat of the day.

By the soft light of a brilliant moon Mr. Hoole's bearers trotted along the narrow tracks called roads in that far-off land, through swamps and jungles, over the hills and across the bridgeless streams. The first river they forded was much swollen by recent rains. The current was strong, and several feet deep. Mr. Hoole wondered how they would get him and his palankeen over it. But those bearers understood their business. Pausing on the bank they took off most of their clothing, which they folded about their heads. Then taking up their load they moved with it into the water up to their knees; then they stood still until the palankeen with its inmate, was placed on the heads of six bearers. Moving on, these men were presently up to their necks in water. Mr. Hoole was, of course, not a little nervous lest the strength of the current should overpower his men. He had heard of parties swept to destruction by a sudden rush of water from the mountains. But, aided by their comrades, who held their hands, they moved steadily forward into shallow water, and the missionary found himself safe on the other side. After eight days of this uncomfortable mode of traveling he reached Negapatam, which, for a brief space, was to be his field for Christian work.

As yet his time was largely spent in the study of the people's language; but, like a faithful worker, he did what he could by preaching through an interpreter. He chose the numerous choultries in the country around the city as preaching places. He always found many people in them. Standing on the steps in their front, with his native interpreter, he spoke to them of Jesus, and found them very ready to listen.

When the time came for him to proceed to his appointment at Bangalore, he made the journey of three hundred miles, borne as before, in a palankeen. It took him thirteen days of discomfort and fatigue to make this trip. He soon learned to preach in Tamul; but, while walking one evening, came very near finishing his work before it was fairly begun. India is a land of venomous serpents, which destroy thousands of lives every year. As he was crossing a hedge one of these animals, about three feet in length, was creeping on the side opposite to him. Fortunately, in leaping the hedge, Mr. Hoole cleared the dangerous creature. Had he leaped upon it, his life would have been sacrificed.

The sights which meet a missionary's eyes in heathen lands are often disgusting, sometimes horrible. Even the religion of those lost ones is cruel. To please their imaginary gods many of them torture themselves. Mr. Hoole saw men in and about Bangalore, some of whom had holes bored through their cheeks and tongues; others had iron or wooden spikes running through those holes; still others stood with lighted fire on their heads; others were there wearing iron frames over a foot square riveted around their necks. One man whom he saw was walking on a pilgrimage with spikes thickly set in the soles of his sandals, his feet pressing on their points. Can you wonder that missionaries who see such sights are so filled with pity as to give up the sweet comforts of home, and to brave perils by sea and land, and to wear themselves into early graves through living in sickly climates?

In this volume I have aimed to give you a peep at some of those dangers and annoyances which make the life of a missionary one of inconveniences and hardships. But these trials are light when compared with the sorrow they feel because of the misery, wickedness, and unwillingness of heathen people to receive the truth. These things burden their hearts and crush their health. But for the success they do witness, which is in truth very great, and the comfort of heavenly love which they enjoy, none of them would live very long. Even with these medicines of the mind many of them soon break down and die. Others when first disabled wisely return to their native land to recruit and to preach to their countrymen at home. Mr. Hoole, after eight years of very hard work, which bore some luxurious fruit, found himself obliged to cease his work and to return to England. Other men entered into his labors, and multitudes in India, once steeped in heathen wretchedness, are now happy men, earnest Methodists, and loyal disciples of our beloved Lord.

Now let us glance at a Wesleyan missionary, named William Shaw, whose field was in South Africa, some three hundred miles from that of Mr. Barnabas Shaw.* His chapel is an old farm-house, in a state of ruin. Its floor is the earth; its thatched roof is much broken; and its reed walls are pierced with holes to let in light and air. His pulpit is a flour barrel with a writing desk on top. The building is infested with rats and mice, which attract the venomous snakes of the country. As the missionary is speaking one day, one of his hearers jumps up and exclaims,

"Sir, there is a puff adder between your feet!"

* See preceding chapter.

Mr. Shaw looks down and sees the deadly creature close to his feet. He quietly steps aside; the people rush upon the snake with sticks and kill it. And thus the missionary narrowly escapes the deadly peril which had met him at his post of duty.

This same gentleman is starting one morning to one of his appointments, seventy miles away from his humble abode. He mounts one horse. His man is astride a second beast, and leads a third by the bridle. He rides briskly for two hours across the lonely country. Then his horse needs rest. He dismounts, rests about twenty or thirty minutes, and then, mounting the led horse, starts again. In some two hours more his horses are languid through thirst and heat. He searches for water. After he finds it, the horses are allowed to drink and rest. Then off he rides again beneath the scorching sun until both horse and rider are parched with thirst. A pool of dirty brackish water is found. The horses dash toward it; but have to be kept from it until they cool off a little. The missionary slakes his thirst as best he can with the distasteful water, then sits down with not so much as a shrub to shelter his burning brain. Opening his portmanteau, he eats the little food it contains. After finishing his scanty luncheon, he looks to the north-west and sees dark clouds rolling across the sky. Knowing that they portend a severe storm, he hastily mounts his weary steed and hurries on.

But the storm is swifter than his horse, and the rain descends in torrents wetting him to the skin. As night approaches he lights upon a lonely farm-house. Pausing at its door-step, he hails the farmer who asks,

"Who are you, if I may ask?"

"I am a missionary. May I saddle off, if you please?"

Consent being given, he and his man enter. A simple meal is given them. He then holds a religious service with the household; after which, as they have no bed to offer him, he lies down on the bare ground and tries to go to sleep, thinking that he has traveled fifty miles that day toward his appointment. But before sleep visits his weary eyes the rain again pours down in torrents upon the leaking roof of the rude dwelling. Every thing is speedily wet; and, tired though he be, he can scarcely close his eyes through the tedious night. His poor tired horses are suffering too outside, for the farmer has no barn, and the beasts stand in the pelting rain without food until morning.

With the dawn of day he starts again, rides two hours, then stops to rest. His man kindles a fire in the open air, boils some water in a tin vessel, steeps some tea, and this, with a little dry bread, is our missionary's breakfast! Again he takes to his saddle and rides on to his appointment. After preaching, meeting class, and seeing his people, he starts to return home. But the rains which met him on his way out have swollen the streams, and without a roof to protect him, he has to wait at the overflowing fords until the water is low enough for him to cross. And then he hastens as he may to his home and family.

This is a specimen of Mr. Shaw's circuit journeys in South Africa. And it was by such hardships as these, that Wesleyan missions were established in South Africa. O much enduring missionaries! What but the love of Christ could move men to face such trials?

CHAPTER XIV.

TWO MISSIONARY PIONEERS IN INDIA.

> "This is our mission; we are blest
>   Obeying holy love's behest;
> In his sweet name we send
>   Glad tidings to the lands afar,
> That rays from our Prophetic star
> With their night shades may blend."
>
> —Mrs. H. B. Crave.

THIRTY years ago our Missionary Society sent out a call for some one to go to India to start a mission. Nearly two years fled into the dead past before any man responded. Then the Rev. William Butler, of the New England Conference, answered the call, saying, "Here am I, send me!"

Believing him to be the right man for the place, the Church authorities bade Dr. Butler go. But this gentleman had four children, two of whom being over seven years old it was not safe to take to so hot a climate. They must be left behind to be educated.

To leave their beloved boys to the care of strangers in a boarding school was a sore trial to Dr. Butler and his excellent wife. Their hearts bled when they bade the little fellows good-bye. But they did it for the sake of Him who once gave his life for their sin—for the sins of the world. One of the dear lads they never saw again. He died before they returned to America.

Steam-ships bore this missionary minister and his family across the great wide sea, first to Europe, and then to India, in safety. After landing at Calcutta they traveled by rail to Lucknow, in the Province of Oudh, where, after due inquiry as to the most suitable place, Mr. Butler determined to begin his mission. It was a city with half a million people in it, and outwardly as "lovely as the outer court of Paradise." But the people were as vile as sin could make them. They were also very unfriendly to foreigners, whose religion they detested with perfect hatred.

That terrible rebellion of the Sepoys, which, made the civilized world sick at heart, was on the point of breaking forth; and such was the bitterness of the natives toward men with white faces, that it was not safe for Dr. Butler to walk the streets of Lucknow without an armed trooper to protect him.

Our missionary called on an officer of the British government and told him that he was about to found a Methodist mission in the city.

"It is madness to attempt it," said this gentleman. "Your life will not be safe if you attempt it. The most sensible thing for you to do is to retrace your steps to Calcutta and take the first ship that sails for America."

Then our undaunted doctor visited Sir James Outram, one of the bravest of old England's brave soldiers, and told him that he was trying to hire a house in Lucknow where he intended to preach the Gospel. The General looked at the missionary with wonder in his eyes, shrugged his shoulders, and told him it would be certain death to stand up in any part of that city or province and preach Jesus.

"It is my duty to preach, Sir James; my Master will take care of my life, and his Spirit will give my preaching success," replied our heroic missionary.

But this bold soldier, who could lead his troops into a deadly breach, could not understand how a missionary could stand alone and unarmed amid thousands of infuriated Mohammedans and Hindus, and utter words sure to make them more furious still. So our missionary and the soldier parted, never to meet again in this world.

No house could be found in Lucknow, and Dr. Butler was obliged to hire one at a place named Bareilly.

Dr. Butler needed a helper who could speak both in English and in the language of the country. He found such a man, who, when an orphan boy, had been reared and taught by the Presbyterian missionaries in their mission school at Allahabad. His name was Joel. His missionary friends, though very fond of Joel, were willing to part with him for the sake of the cause of truth, provided the young man was disposed to go with Dr. Butler, who said to him,

"Joel, I am going to start a mission at Bareilly, three hundred miles away from your friends. I want a helper. Will you go with me?"

Yes, Joel was willing, but he had a wife, a lovely young creature, and a little babe. Perhaps she would not consent to leave her mother. He would ask her.

Emma, his brave little wife, nobly replied, "I will go whither you go, if my mother will consent."

Dr. Butler knew that Peggy, Emma's mother, loved her daughter very fondly. He was almost afraid to ask her to make such a sacrifice as was involved in letting her go. Hence he went with Joel to see her, feeling very doubtful as to the results.

Peggy listened to the request which the

doctor was so loth to make. It drew tears from her eyes, but with a heroism born of her loving faith, she replied,

"Sahib, (sir,) the Saviour came down from heaven to give himself for me, and why should not I give my daughter to his work?"

O, noble Peggy! Though born an idolater she had believed in Christ through missionary teaching; and her loving faith had transformed her into a Christian heroine.

Joel and Emma went to Bareilly with Dr. Butler. It soon appeared that, though Joel could repeat his Catechism and read his Bible, he did not know what it was to be "born again." But being honest and sincere, as soon as he learned that Christianity was both a doctrine and an experience, he sought the experience, and in a short time was filled with the love of Christ. He then became a helper indeed to Dr. Butler, and in due time preached the Gospel to his countrymen. Joel was the first native Methodist preacher in our Indian Mission.

Dr. Butler had scarcely set up his "household goods" in Bareilly before the terrible Sepoy rebellion burst forth, terrible as a tornado. "You must take your women and children to the hills *at once*," was the notice sent him by the British officer in command. He hated to quit his post. So did his heroic wife. But warning after warning to leave came to him, and after holding his ground three or four days, he concluded to heed those warning voices and flee to the mountains. Joel being a native, thought himself safe, and promised to stay at Bareilly and do what he could to keep up the work and guard the property of the infant mission.

Their flight began in the night. They had before them a journey of seventy-four miles up the hills to Nynee Tal,* where they hoped to be in safety until the rebellion should be overcome. For twenty miles of that distance their road ran through a jungle thick with trees, reeking with malaria, and the haunt of wild elephants and

* See Frontispiece.

ferocious tigers. They traveled at night by the dim light of flickering torches. To make matters worse, at midnight of their second night's travel, many of the doctor's palankeen bearers forsook him. Others refused to proceed. He was now in deadly peril of perishing in the wilderness. His heart sunk within him. He could only do one thing more, and that he did. He stepped within the jungle where, standing bareheaded, he pleaded with God to incline his obstinate bearers to go forward. Did Heaven answer that prayer? It did; for, on returning to his palankeen, he found them docile and making preparation to move on. The next morning he reached the traveler's bungalow, where he and his family tasted food for the first time during twenty-two hours of tedious and perilous travel. One more journey of seven hours took them into Nynee Tal, a sanitarium situated in the bosom of the mountains, where, in a little furnished cottage, they found rest from their toil and, as they hoped, comparative safety from the rebellious Sepoys.

But what became of Joel and Emma? Did they live in peace in Bareilly? By no means. The Sepoys, after destroying every thing belonging to the English residents and to Dr. Butler at Bareilly, sought to kill every native Christian they could find. Warned in time of his danger, Joel, with his delicate little wife, sought safety in flight. They escaped, but their sufferings during their wanderings on foot, three hundred and forty miles, were at times almost too great for endurance. But, thanks to Heaven's watchful providence, and to the brave Havelock and his troops, whom they me ton their march to Lucknow, they found safety at last in Allahabad!

But Dr. Butler and his family were not yet beyond the reach of the murderous Sepoys, who prepared to send a force to destroy the refugees who had gathered at Nynee Tal. Warned of these preparations, the British authorities directed that the ladies, with a few gentlemen to protect them, should be sent thirty miles farther, to a place named Almorah. Our much-tried missionary was deputed to be one of the gentlemen to go with this party. The road was steep, narrow, rough, and very dangerous. It took three days' travel to reach their comfortless place of refuge. Dr. Butler, through the fall of the pony on which he rode, narrowly escaped being thrown into the deep gorge which lay on one side of this mountain road. But Heaven again preserved his life, and he and his noble wife were permitted, after the suppression of the rebellion, to retrace their steps to Bareilly, and, in connection with additional missionaries from home, who had already arrived in India, to lay again the foundation of a mission. Disaster had met the first attempt. Dr. Butler's library and goods had been destroyed, but being sustained by faith and hope, he and his noble fellow-workers gave themselves to their work, and succeeded in planting one of the most important and successful missions of modern times. The doctor formed the first class in Bareilly with seven members, in May, 1857. To-day, April 8, 1884, the North India Conference, of which that class was the germ, numbers 900 preachers, teachers, and helpers, 4,662 members, 6,679 adherents, and 16,705 Sunday-school scholars. Behold, what hath God wrought!

FIRST METHODIST EPISCOPAL CHURCH IN INDIA.

India owes a heavy debt to the self-denying pioneers of our missions in North India. There is also another moral hero, whose work wrought precious results among the Eurasians, or East Indians as they prefer being called, in Southern India. These are persons whose fathers were

Europeans and whose mothers were natives of India. They form a very respectable and useful element in Indian society. The gentleman whose labors have brought them great and manifold spiritual blessings is the Rev. WILLIAM TAYLOR, whose remarkable zeal for his Lord has given him a world-wide and honorable fame. His first success as an evangelist was won in California, and then throughout the United States. A pious Canadian, who knew of his success in California, spoke to him one day about the needs of Australia. "I will go thither," said he. In keeping this purpose he went through parts of England, Ireland, and Palestine, preaching Jesus. Next he won many to Christ in Australia and New Zealand. He then sailed to South Africa, where thousands of colonists and native Kaffirs were given him as fruits of his preaching.

With unresting zeal he afterward went to the West India Islands, to British Guiana, and then, on the invitation of our India Conference missionaries, to India.

After preaching with fair results in several large cities, Mr. Taylor, in November, 1871, began to hold special services in Bombay. Conversions followed. But his plain dealing and energetic methods were distasteful to the ministers and churches in that city. Then this earnest man said within himself,

"These ministers and churches will not so treat my converts as to nurse them into earnest working Christians. I will, therefore, form them into Fellowship Bands."

With Mr. Taylor a good purpose means instant and decided action. Hence the bands were formed, somewhat after the pattern of Mr. Wesley's first societies. But the members of these bands, desiring closer fellowship with each other, soon asked Mr. Taylor to organize them into a Methodist Episcopal Church. He yielded to their wishes, and organized them according to our Discipline, they agreeing to make the Church "evangelistic, *self-supporting*, and without distinction of language, caste, or color."

Out of this humble beginning the South India Conference speedily grew. Mr. Taylor, after raising up bands of converts in other cities, accepted some helpers from among his converts, and sent to America for others. As all his infant churches agreed to support their ministers without help from America, our Missionary Society only paid the passages of such brethren as responded to Mr. Taylor's call. Those helpers were every-where successful in forming churches. No similar work of such magnitude as this, so soon attained, has been accomplished in modern times at such small expense to the mother Church. The South India Conference, with its three Presiding Elders' districts, stands to-day a grand monument to the heroic courage, the remarkable self-denial, the deep piety, the unshrinking faith of William Taylor. He has since been engaged in an attempt to repeat this success in South America, where both circumstances and people seem very different from those in India. Possibly the difficulties there are insurmountable. Possibly his manifold resources, his personal power with men, and his fearless faith in God may overcome them, and a self-supporting Methodist Episcopal Church be established in·that priest-ridden country. We hope it may be done. Be this as it may, William Taylor's name will go down to the ages as that of a man whose courage, zeal, and usefulness entitle him to the admiration and love of all who love the souls of men and the cause of the Lord Jesus Christ.

Bishop Taylor.

Since the above was written the missionary ability of William Taylor has been most emphatically recognized by our Church in his election as a Missionary Bishop for Africa! The state of our work in Liberia has for some time past demanded more Episcopal service then could possibly be suppplied by the Board of Bishops. Although the Liberia Mission has been of incalculable value to many within its narrow bounds, it has not accomplished such results on the neighboring nations as to satisfy the desires of our Church. God is evidently forcing the needs of that great and populous country on the attention of the world, and it may be truthfully said that "Ethiopia is stretching out her hands unto God." It must also be accepted as a sign of the times that, when our late General Conference was electing Bishops, there sprang up a strong desire to place a Bishop in Africa, whose life-work it should be to spread our work over that continent. And when the hour came to select a man, the thought of a large majority of the body settled, almost spontaneously, on William Taylor. He was accordingly elected and ordained to be our Bishop for Africa. Bowing to the will of the Church, as indicating the will of God, he accepts the office. He goes into the perils of that sickly climate fully aware of its risks and responsibilities. But he goes fearlessly and hopefully, knowing that the God of Missions, who has been with him in the past, will be with him there also. He believes in success through the prayers of the Church and the help of the

Holy Ghost It is to be presumed that the General Missionary Committee will make him a liberal appropriation with which to start his work; and that after stirring up the slumbering energies of the Liberia Conference, he will push out into the regions beyond its lines. There is said to be a vast plateau in Central Africa where numerous tribes abound, and where the climate is so healthy as not to be fatal to white men. of such a place is to be found, he will surely find it. Who that reads these lines will not breathe an earnest prayer, saying, "O God, bless the labors of Bishop Taylor in the dark continent of Africa!"

CHAPTER XV.

SOME HEROIC LADY MISSIONARIES.

> "My soul is not at rest; there comes a strange
>   And secret whisper to my spirit, like
> A dream at night, that tells me I am on
>   Enchanted grounds. Why live I here? The vows
> Of God are on me, and I may not stoop
>   To play with shadows, or pluck earthly flowers,
> Till I my work have done, and rendered up account."
> —Dr. Nathan Brown.

IN India and China there are millions of girls and women who, because of the ways of the people, can only be taught to know Jesus by lady teachers. Gentleman missionaries cannot reach them as they do ignorant women in this country. That Christian ladies might be sent to do this work, a society of Methodist ladies was formed at Boston, in 1869. It looks like a perilous work for single young women to leave their native land, and sail thousands of miles to a strange and trying climate, to live with a strange people for the sole purpose of telling them the old, old story of the blessed Redeemer's love for the souls of men and women. Well, it is a very great thing for any young lady to undertake. It requires great faith, much love, rare courage, and genuine loyalty to Christ and to the perishing heathen for whom he died. But great as are the sacrifices this holy work demands, this "Women's Foreign Missionary Society" has never lacked accomplished young women willing to undertake it.

The first money given to this Society came from a lady whose daughter, when dying, said to her mother, "If I do not get well I would like to have papa give as much money to the missionaries every year as it requires to take care of me." That sweet girl passed into the "Beautiful Land," and her mother, in honor of her memory, gave the first offering made to the Society "for the support of a Bible woman in Moradabad, India." Thus, by her dying wish, that lovely maiden not only encouraged the ladies of the Society, but also caused many to hear the words of Christ in India who had never before known even his glorious name.

This Society was scarcely organized before an accomplished lady, Miss I. Thoburn, whose heart had been a fountain of desire to work among the women of India, offered to bear its banner to the zenanas of India. The ladies had but three hundred dollars in their treasury. This sum was only sufficient for her outfit. The ladies felt sad at heart, and for some moments looked at each other in silent despair. Presently one of their number, Mrs. Edwin F. Porter, as if suddenly moved by the Holy Spirit, rose and spoke with a spiritual force which made her words arrows of celestial fire. At the close of her spontaneous address, which was like an inspiration, speaking of Miss Thoborn, she used these memorable words:

"Shall we lose her because we have not the needed money in our hands? No; rather let us walk the streets of Boston in our calico robes and save the expense of more costly apparel. Mrs. President, I move the appointment of Miss Thoburn as our missionary to India."

These were noble words, and the ladies replied, as with one voice, "We will send her!" The response was not the expression of an ungrounded, empty enthusiasm, but of a faith which rested on God's promises to bless the efforts of his Son's followers. Ladies who were ready to wear calico instead of silk, if that were necessary to the procurement of money, were justified in pledging themselves to the support of Miss Thoburn in India.

That they made no mistake in this their first missionary, Miss Thoburn's work in India abundantly proves. She was well educated; she had the tastes and aspirations of a lady of culture; she loved the refinements of civilized life; she was full of energy, and was devoted to the service of her Lord. All this she consecrated to the women of India. She organized schools for girls; she visited the zenanas to tell their inmates about Jesus; she made herself beloved and very useful. After she had spent several years of toil in India, she was asked by an American lady who was visiting her field of labor,

"Do you not sometimes long for your own land of privilege?"

Her reply deserves to be embroidered on cloth of gold. With features all aglow with heavenly fire, she said, "Don't go home to excite pity for me! I am happy here in my work. I am busy here, and we all feel so. Our work lies here; and when sickness comes, and we turn our faces homeward, we leave our hearts behind."

This was the language of a genuine missionary, working for Jesus out of pure love for the souls in whose behalf he died. Nor was she the only heroic lady willing to give up home and its delights from the same great motive. There was MISS CLARA A. SWAIN, who accompanied her. This lady had studied medicine, and she sailed with Miss Thoburn as a medical missionary. She did good service until her failing health compelled her to return with reluctance to her native land.

Miss Fannie J. Sparkes, a young lady of Binghamton, N. Y., nurtured in a home of love, and well educated, when converted, in 1869, heard a whisper in her heart asking, "Will you go to India, alone, as a missionary for Jesus?"

To this startling question, after severe struggles of mind, she finally answered, "Yes." Shortly after Mr. Judd, a returned missionary, asked her if she would go to India. Her pastor, her presiding elder, and the ladies of the Missionary Society, pressed the same inquiry. These wishes of her earthly friends satisfied her that the whisper in her heart was from her beloved Lord. Still there was the unwillingness of her parents to part with her yet to be overcome. They loved her with tender affection. Her heart was bound to theirs, and while they hesitated to give their consent, she suffered intensely. Jesus bade her go. Her parents wished her to stay at home. Whom did she love best? Jesus gained the victory, and her parents withdrew their opposition for his sake. She sailed to Bombay, and having arrived safely, she was sent to Bareilly to take charge of a Girls' Orphanage. There she did "grand and glorious work," teaching many native orphan girls the knowledge of the truth as it is in Jesus.

Eight years of faithful labor in a trying climate wore out her strength, and compelled her return to her native land. Great was the joy of her friends when she reached her father's home. After his first greeting, that happy father said, "Let us sing 'Praise God, from whom all blessings flow;'" and the assembled household sang it with a joyousness that may be more easily imagined than described.

Eighteen months at home restored her strength, despite the labor of speaking at one hundred missionary meetings in various parts of the country. Then she returned to her much-loved Orphanage in Bareilly. Her farewell words before sailing were pitched to a lofty and heroic key-note. She said, "Saying good-bye is not all sacrifice. There is so much joy in the thought of carrying the light of life to heathen women, that had I a thousand lives, I would gladly lay them all upon the altar of this service."

Most noble lady, what generous mind can refuse to honor thee for these truly heroic words!

There is in the cemetery at Binghamton, N. Y., a tombstone bearing this simple inscription: "Nellie; died at sea, aged 21 years." Beneath are the words, "She hath done what she could." Who was this youthful lady who, though young when translated to heaven, had "done what she could?"

She was one of our lady missionaries to China, the wife of the Rev. S. L. Baldwin, whose missionary record will be written on the chief corner-stone of the coming Chinese Methodist Episcopal Church. When Nellie became his bride she cheerfully accepted the perils and sacrifices of the work to which he was self-consecrated. Her devotion to her chosen vocation was beautifully shown the last time she knelt at the paternal family altar. As the farewell prayer went from quivering lips to the ears of our elder Brother in heaven, every eye but Nellie's was filled with tears. Rising from her knees she quietly seated herself at the piano, and in a voice made clear and strong by the inspiration of faith and love, she sang,

> " Yes, my native land, I love thee!
> All thy scenes I love them well;
> Friends, connections, happy country,
> Can I bid you all farewell;
> Can I leave you,
> Far in heathen lands to dwell."

This sweet singer was only nineteen years old. Yet she was no mere sentimentalist, but a pure young soul intelligently consecrated to Christian work in China. What she did after arriving at Foochow proved, beyond all question, that she was speaking in earnest when shortly after the above scene around the family altar she uttered her last words in America, saying, " I do not regret the step I have taken. I go cheerfully, fully determined to do all the good I can." This high purpose she executed, quickly acquiring the language of the people, and heartily entering into her husband's labors. But less than two years sufficed to sap the sources of her strength, and compel her to take ship for her native land. She passed from the great wide sea to her reward when the vessel was six days from port. Her earthly career was brief but beautiful, and her rest is glorious.

Let us now view the father of a sick, motherless infant, kneeling alone in his chamber and fervently praying. "Spare the life of my child, O Lord!" he cries, "If thou wilt save her, I dedicate her to thy service as a missionary to heathen lands."

Heaven kindly answered that father's prayer. The life of his beloved child was given him. Her name was CARRIE L. M'MILLAN. Very singularly, as she grew up and while she was yet a little girl, she secretly cherished the thought that her life-work was to be done in India. And when she began to study geography, and to trace on the map the ocean paths to India and the location of the great cities of the eastern world, she did so, thinking,

"My school-mates and teachers little think I shall see those places."

When only seven years old she was happily converted. Then her love for the Saviour became the root of a fond undying desire to realize her inward thought. And when she blossomed into young womanhood, she told these secret longings to her pastor and his wife, who, knowing her fitness for missionary work, took the proper steps to bring her name before the directors of our Woman's Missionary Society.

While her case was pending, her father told her, for the first time, of his prayer for her infant life, and of the dedication he then made of her life to missionary work. And he added,

"I hope, Carrie, you will yet live to fulfill this vow!"

Then this girl, whose heart was already overflowing with desire for work among the heathen, rejoiced with exceeding joy. She saw the connection between her fond father's prayer and her missionary longings. She was satisfied that her long-cherished thought was a seed sown by the chief of Missionaries, even by Christ the Lord.

She was appointed in due time. Then came the test of her devotion. To quit her home-nest, where a father's love had brightened her young life, and to venture, a defenseless maiden, across the measureless sea into a strange land was a sterner thing to do than it had been to imagine in her young day-dreams. Her father also found it a bitter trial to say adieu to his consecrated child. His heart shrunk from it as from a living death. But he said it, though it was with anguish that cannot be told. After it was said and his loved daughter had left to take ship, he poured out his grief into the ear of his sympathizing Lord. Nor did he do this in vain. The Spirit comforted him, and when he left his place of prayer his face was radiant with the light of God's face, and he said to his son,

"I have gained the victory! Glory, glory! I am glad Carrie is gone, and glad she has such a message to deliver!"

This devoted lady entered zealously and successfully on her work of teaching Jesus. The secret of her success was made clear by what she wrote back to her friends, "Of my work in India," said she, "*I love it.* I love the people with a peculiar love. I am glad I have a place in this field. I am glad that prayer for India's redemption is being answered. The time is coming when India's daughters, so long bound by the fetters of superstition, shall hear the voice of Christ. The door of the zenana shall swing back, and in the light of God's countenance they shall come forth."

These are words of love and faith. These are the forces that move both men and women to face the trials of mission work. And by these the world shall be won to our Christ.

One more sketch from the portrait gallery of our "Woman's Foreign Missionary Society" is all we have to insert in this chapter. It is that of Miss Susan B. Higgins, the daughter of a devout Methodist preacher, a graduate of the High School at Chelsea, Massachusetts, and subsequently a very superior teacher in the public schools of Boston. When sixteen years old she became one of our Lord's disciples. As his follower she could not help thinking much of missionary work, and she was much inclined, when missionary collections were being taken, to write, "*I give myself.*" But her native modesty kept her from doing so.

At last, after much self-scrutiny, hesitation, and fear, lest she should ever go without being sent, she made up her mind to offer herself. In this state of mind she went to a quarterly meeting of the society where, at the close of its session, a lady who knew her worth remarked to her, "I think we will send you as a missionary sometime."

"*Any time,*" promptly replied Miss Higgins' with an emphasis that led the lady to look intently into her eyes, and to rejoin,

"Apply, then; apply!"

She went home in very thoughtful mood. Her room-mate met her with the inquiry, "Susan, are you going to be a missionary?"

"I am going to apply," was her decisive answer.

She did apply, but there was no vacancy. She would have to wait for an opening. The resignation of a lady recently appointed, however, soon opened a door for her. She was appointed to Yokohama.

Then came the tender farewells, the long voyage, the hopes and fears of a sensitive Christian lady on entering upon a novel and difficult task. All these trials she passed with courage and hope. Her success was assured from the beginning. The Japanese children, won by her Christian gentleness, soon loved her. Her prospect was bright with promise when, after less than a year of devoted labor, she was seized with sudden sickness. Her physician frankly said,

"You may get well, but it is very doubtful."

"I am in the Lord's hands," she replied, very calmly. "Living or dying, I am his."

It was her Lord's good pleasure to take her

to his upper sanctuary, and she died with a song of triumph on her faltering tongue.

O, noble Christian maiden! Her brow is crowned with glory to day, and her example lives to fire other kindred young souls with that heroic zeal which promptly fills every gap made by disease and death in the ranks of our missionaries.

Would the reader know more of the elect ladies who have been sent abroad by the Woman's Foreign Missionary Society? Let him read Mrs. Wheeler's book on the subject.

CHAPTER XVI.

MISSIONARY SCENES AND INCIDENTS.

> "Keep thou Zionward thy face,
>   Ask in faith the aid of grace,
> Use the strength which grace shall give,
>   Die to self—in Christ to live."
>
> —BERNARD BARTON.

IN 1873 sixty persons were assembled on a Sabbath day in a hall at Modena, Italy. A Christian Italian, named Signor A. Guigon, preached a sermon. Dr. Vernon, our pioneer missionary to Italy, followed him with an address, giving the reasons why American Methodism had made its appearance in that country. This was the opening scene in the history of the Italian Methodist Episcopal Church. It was not an imposing spectacle; nevertheless, as the tiny acorn grows into the future majestic oak, so, from this humble beginning, our Church expects to become a mighty energy in the hand of

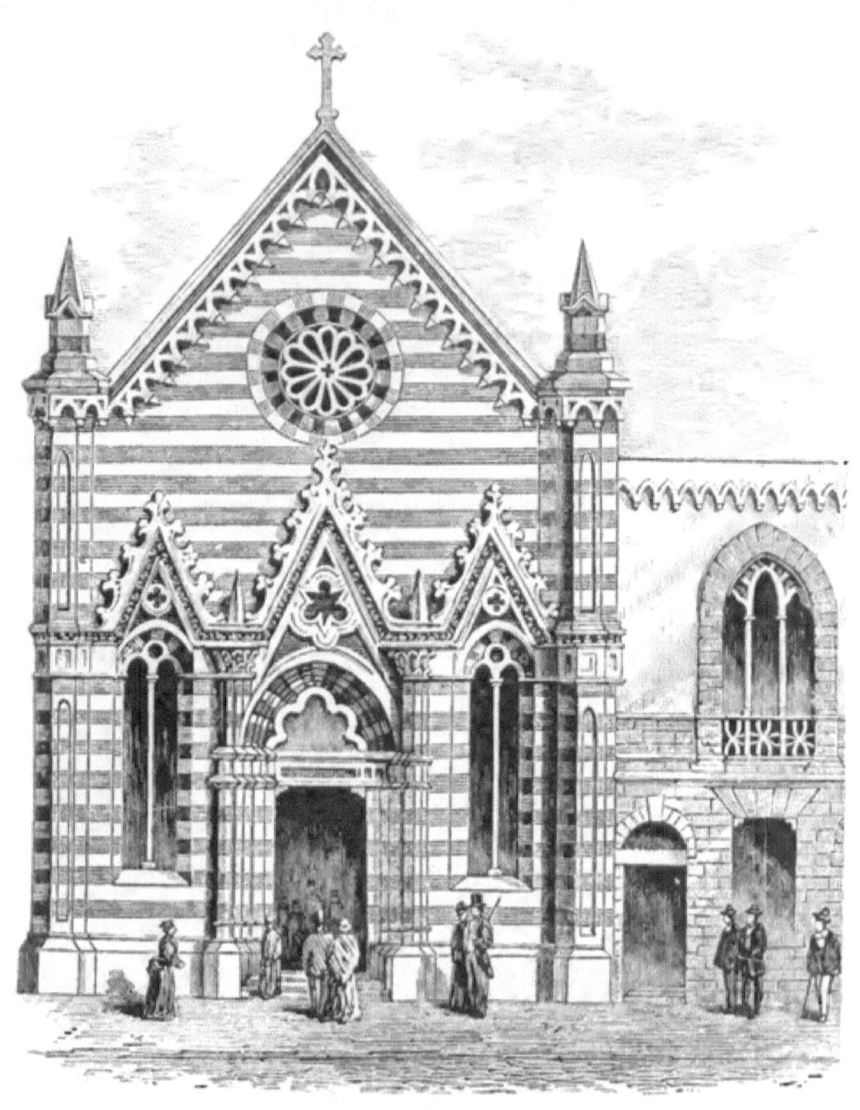

St. Paul's Methodist Episcopal Church, Rome.

God in the regeneration of that land of beauty and of song.

In Rome, in 1875, on Christmas-day, another scene was witnessed by the angry Romanist priests of that proud city. This was nothing less than the dedication of St. Paul's Methodist Episcopal Church in the Via Polo—the first Italian Protestant Church in Rome. The building was crowded. The Pope, cardinals, monks, and priests were filled with impotent rage at being compelled to behold a Protestant edifice for the use of native citizens standing on ground once owned by them—a fact which through long centuries they had been able to prevent by the power of the sword. But the providence of God, by giving civil and religious freedom to a united Italy, had now made such an edifice possible. Dr. Vernon dedicated this beautiful little church; and three Italian Methodist traveling preachers preached in its pulpit on that eventful Christmas-day. The significance of this fact was seen in the stir it created throughout the city. While the papal authorities gnashed their teeth, the friends of liberty rejoiced; the press was jubilant; and the telegraphic wire bore the glad tidings, not only through, but beyond, the kingdom of Italy, to Paris and London.

So remarkable was the presence of this church in the "eternal city," that Dr. Vernon subsequently said, "Often while meditating within this bright little church, I ask myself, 'Is this real, here where until the autumn of 1870 the papal pall hung over all, dark and dark as the shadow of death?'" Well, it is real; and if saints in heaven are made acquainted with the progress of the Church on earth, the unnumbered souls of martyrs whose bodies were tortured to death by the cruel persecutions authorized by the Roman *curia*, must drink in fresh draughts of joy as they fall before the throne and thank the Redeemer for this sign of the coming, final overthrow of the "man of sin."

Let us now pass in imagination from the city of the Pope to the capital city of Mexico, on our own continent. In this latter city the simple-minded Montezuma once reigned in all the splendor of a semi-civilized monarch. His palace was an immense and costly structure. It had long been the home of the Aztec kings. More than three hundred years ago the greedy, blood-thirsty Spaniards, led by the conquering Cortez, fought their way to the conquest of this city. Not content with the submission of Montezuma to their power, those ruthless Spaniards, their priests especially, looked with a covetous eye on the palace and treasures of the fallen king. Regardless of right and honor, they ousted the unfortunate Montezuma from the house of his ancestors and seized his country, his palace, and his riches in the name of the Spanish king and of the Pope. The Romish priests soon took possession of the palace, changed it into a vast monastery, which they filled with monks imported from Spain, and made it the head-quarters of their movements for bringing the Mexicans into submission to their creed. By robbing the people of their lands and treasure they made this monastery of San Francisco, as they named it, immensely rich. At one time they kept four thousand monks in idleness and luxury within its walls; but the Mexican people, under their priestly rule, though ceasing to be idolaters after their old Aztec fashion, gained little religious benefit by the change. They were ignorant idolaters still, though their idols bore the names of Mary, St. Peter, and other Christian saints. The rule of Rome in Mexico was never a blessing, but a perpetual curse to its people.

No; not a *perpetual* curse. There came a time, not many years ago, when, wearied with both kingcraft and priestly rule, the Mexicans shot their king, created the Mexican republic, and confiscated the stolen estates of the priests for the benefit of the nation.

In 1873 Bishop Haven and Dr. Wm. Butler went to emancipated, but still spiritually blind, Mexico to establish Methodism. Going to its chief city they found portions of the confiscated Convent of St. Francisco in the market. It had been divided into lots. Its central part, including cloisters and a beautiful court, had been leased and turned into a circus for the entertainment of the public. It was, however, well adapted for a mission house and church. Hence, the Bishop and Dr. Butler made overtures for its purchase. The priests set themselves to keep this former seat of their power from being sold for Methodistic purposes. It required both skill and patience to overcome their hostile measures. But this was accomplished at last. Our Church purchased the title, fitted up a beautiful church, a printing-office, and preacher's home on the chief seat of ancient Aztec royalty and of Romanistic priestcraft in the city of Mexico. On Christmas-day, 1873, this edifice, so long devoted in its old shape to the interests of the kingdom of darkness, was solemnly dedicated, in the presence of six hundred interested spectators, to the religion of Christ as understood and enjoyed by the Methodist Episcopal Church. Was not this a victory, not so much for our Church as for the Christ and for the best interests of the Mexican people?

Romanism never hesitates to shed Christian blood where it has the power. Its history is symbolized by the scarlet cloaks of its cardinals; and were it in full possession of the government in these United States, it would, without doubt, stain the pavements of our city parks with the blood of martyrs. Its unchanged character was shown in Mexico when the missionaries of our own and other Christian Churches began to win converts to the true faith. Hence our missionaries had scarcely completed their preparations for evangelical work before they were warned that a society of Roman Catholics had been formed in Mexico for the purpose of killing our superintendent and other missionaries, with some distinguished Protestant laymen. This murderous spirit was not confined to the city of Mexico, but showed itself in other places where missionaries of our Church and of other Christian bodies had begun to teach the pure truth. That these breathings of slaughter meant actual murder was proven by riotous assaults on churches in several cities, and by the killing of at least twenty of Christ's disciples, in the space of little more than a year. One word of authority from the chief priests of Romanism in Mexico would have prevented these murderous proceedings. That word was not spoken. But the emancipated Mexican press did speak, boldly charging the Romish Church with responsibility for these villainous deeds. Another voice was heard also. It spoke from Washington, warning the civil authorities in Mexico that they must protect the lives and property of American missionaries. These voices were effectual. The Roman priests saw that by fostering mobs and murders they were sowing dragon's teeth which might produce an army before which they and their institutions might become as chaff driven by a fierce wind. Hence, though they still stir the hatred of their people against our missionaries, they now rarely excite them, at least not openly, to deeds of death. Nevertheless, their evil spirit is kept alive in their ignorant followers, and knowing that it may at any time produce sudden explosions, our missionaries labor, conscious that they are in constant peril of falling at their posts. But they toil on, trusting in their Master, ready to serve him either in life or death. Surely, they are moral heroes! By them and their successors Mexico will assuredly be conquered for the Redeemer.

Our next scene is in a plain Methodist Episcopal Church in Danville, Ohio. It is Sabbath evening. Adam Poe, the presiding elder of the district, has been preaching. The audience is deeply impressed. God is manifestly in their midst. Twenty souls are at the altar. They cry to the Lord, who answers their prayers and fills their believing souls with his pardoning love. They fill the house with shouts of praise, all but one of them. That one is evidently a German, a young man apparently about twenty-eight years of age. The pale cast of thought is on his devout face. A cloud of settled sadness is on his well-developed brow. When the meeting closes he slowly rises from his knees, and, with a heavy heart, moves away toward the door. When his foot touches the threshold he pauses, casts a lingering look on the rejoicing converts, who seem loth to quit the spot on which their Lord admitted them to his fellowship. As he stands gazing on their joy his manner suddenly changes. A new light flashes from his tearful eyes. He presses his way back through the slowly departing crowd to a corner of the church. There he kneels, prays for a few moments, then rises, his face ablaze with the glory of a great inward joy, and with a loud voice shouts forth the praises of his Redeemer's love.

What produced this sudden change in the young man's manner and condition of mind? It was the effect of a blessed thought whispered in his heart by the unseen Spirit of his Lord. While he stood gazing at the rejoicing converts, thinking of his long previous and thus far ineffectual search for the Pearl they had just found, the invisible One moved him to ask, "Is there not bread enough in my Father's house?" With that inquiry there came such a conception of the fullness and sufficiency of the merits of Christ, that to doubt, as he had long done, seemed no longer possible. With that vision before his mental eyes, of Christ's ability to save even him, he had kneeled and prayed, looking alone on the infinite merits of Jesus. While in that solemn act he had suddenly felt relieved of the burden on his conscience. He was filled with such a sense of divine forgiveness and of the love of Christ that his heart overflowed into loud expressions of praise and gladness.

But why dwell on this young man's conversion rather than on that of the others? Because there was a far greater significance in it than in theirs. I do not mean to him or to them personally, but to the world. That young man was no ordinary character. He was destined to be Heaven's instrument in bringing many of his countrymen to the knowledge of the truth. His name was WILLIAM NAST, the father of Methodism among the Germans.

Shall I give you a few points in his early history? He was born in Germany, nurtured by devout parents in the doctrines and worship of the Lutheran Church, and, when fourteen years old, converted and impressed with a burning desire to prepare himself to become a missionary in foreign lands. His parents, desirous to have him enter the ministry of the national Church, sent him first to a preparatory academy, and then to the University of Tubingen. In these institutions he acquired a high degree of scholarship; but, owing to the skeptical teaching of Professor Bauer, and to close associations with Strauss, his classmate, he made shipwreck of the faith which had filled his heart in his youthful days. Therefore, when he bade adieu to the classic halls of Tubingen, he abandoned his former purpose to enter the ministry, and resolved to devote himself to the study of art, science, and polite literature.

But having once tasted the love of Christ, his heart refused to be satisfied with mere literary food. He became as unresting as a vessel on a wind-swept sea; and, hoping to find abroad the repose he could not gain at home, he sailed for New York in 1828, when he was twenty-one years of age, secretly resolved to become a better man.

This resolution remained like a seed on dry ground for a year. Then his watchful Father in heaven directed his steps to the mansion of a lady in Pennsylvania, whom he served as tutor to her family. This elect lady was a member of the Methodist Episcopal Church. In her house he met Methodist preachers. Their conversation and the spirit of her sanctified home revived his early convictions and prepared him, when he removed to West Point to teach German, as he did after a year, to receive deep impressions from two devout young officers who had been converted under the preaching of the chaplain of that military post.

His convictions grew deeper under the sermons of James H. Rowe, stationed at West Point, and through the reading of religious books. A sermon preached by Dr. Fisk, at the annual examination of the cadets, added to his seriousness, but it was not until he attended a camp-meeting on the banks of the Juniata, in

1832, that the utmost depths of his heart were broken up. His penitence was then profound, but either through the peculiar structure of his mind or some misconception of the nature of faith, though he stood forth bravely as Christ's disciple, he did not attain a clear and abiding sense of his acceptance in Christ until on the memorable occasion before described. From that time William Nast's faith was such as to make him in name and deed "a man in Christ."

Some time prior to this delightful experience a venerable mother in Israel, while suffering what seemed to be a mortal sickness, had said to the then despondent Mr. Nast:

"Be of good cheer and praise the Lord. He has chosen you to bear the Gospel message to your countrymen. Thousands of Germans will be saved through your instrumentality!"

This remark was prophetic, though at the time it was made William Nast scarcely dared to hope for his own salvation, much less to regard himself as God's chosen vessel to convey good tidings to others. But now that he was made one with Christ by a living faith, he began to feel the impulses of desire to pluck his fellow-countrymen as brands from the burning. Hence he took steps to enter our ministry; and, being admitted to a Conference and appointed to Cincinnati as German missionary in 1835, he made his appearance in that busy city, where many people from his native land had settled.

His reception among those Germans was not encouraging. Those of them who belonged to the Lutheran Church were mere formalists, who regarded spiritual religion as fanaticism. Others, not of any church, were utterly indifferent to the truths of the Gospel. Mr. Nast had no church especially set apart for their use. His heart burned with desire to do them good, but he was among them as a lonely lamp surrounded by icebergs. Yet he did what he could, holding services for Germans in the English-speaking churches and in halls. He also preached to them in the streets, gave them tracts, and visited them at their homes. Nevertheless, despite all his patient, prayerful labor, he could only report at the end of a year three converts and twenty-three serious souls, of whom twelve met in class.

The friends of the German work in Cincinnati were discouraged, and the next year the Bishop sent our patient toiler to form a circuit over a space which extended three hundred miles, and embraced many towns and cities which had Germans among their populations. Over this wide extent of country our patient itinerant moved monthly, scattering good seed which, though not immediately productive, sprang up at length and brought forth a blessed harvest of German Methodist churches.

After one year of such wide-spread labor, Cincinnati again called for Mr. Nast. He returned, repeated his efforts, secured a German chapel, and before the year expired rejoiced over a little German Methodist Episcopal Church numbering thirty-six members.

Encouraged by this partial success, the friends of the German work rallied round Mr. Nast, and furnished funds for publishing a German paper, tracts, and books, to the editing of which he gave much of his time, besides preaching wherever he found opportunity in and around Cincinnati.

One Sabbath evening, in 1839, a young German physician, finely educated, but by no means religiously inclined, sat near the pulpit in which Mr. Nast was to preach. When Mr. Nast took his text, this proud young worldling said to himself:

"I will look that preacher right in the face and see if I cannot make him laugh."

Then, gazing intently on Mr. Nast, he became so interested in his topic that he soon forgot his idle and wicked purpose. Presently the preacher said,

"There may be a Saul among us whom God will convert into a Paul."

This remark was God's arrow. It went straight to the young physician's heart and inflicted a wound which none but the divine Physician could heal. Happily the young man looked to the great Healer of souls, found remission of sins, joined the Methodist Episcopal Church, and became, under God, the father of the Methodist Episcopal Church in Germany. His name was Ludwig S. Jacoby.

The above-mentioned prophecy of the mother in Israel respecting Nast was now in a fair way to be fulfilled. His labors had already laid the foundation of our German work in America; and by bringing Mr. Jacoby into the Church he had provided instrumentally the man destined to be the founder of our Church in his fatherland. The seed sowed so patiently by the modest William Nast has grown and become a glorious harvest—in two countries. Surely God crowned this good man's missionary work with abundant honors!

We will now turn our attention once more to India and take a peep at the incidents of our missionary work in that country. They are gathered from an excellent work by Rev. Dr. T. J. Scott.

Near the village of Majea, Dr. Scott heard of a famous fakir, whose abode was in a tomb which held the ashes of a man and of his widow who, in the days when the rite of *suttee* flourished, was burned alive with his dead body. There were fifty such tombs in the grove, which was surrounded by a thick matted hedge of thorns. Here the old fakir had lived a hermit life some thirty years. Dr. Scott determined to see him. Having, by a mere chance, found the only path by which his retreat could be reached, he entered it, and saw a venerable looking old man with long unkempt gray hair and beard. His only covering was a black, coarse blanket thrown over one shoulder and drawn round under the other arm. He was moving about looking like a "grim goblin." The missionary hailed him, saying, " Peace on you, old man!"

"Who are you?" responded the devotee with gruff surprise.

"Who am I?" rejoined the doctor.

"Yes, who are you, thrusting yourself in here?"

This was said savagely, but Dr. Scott replied

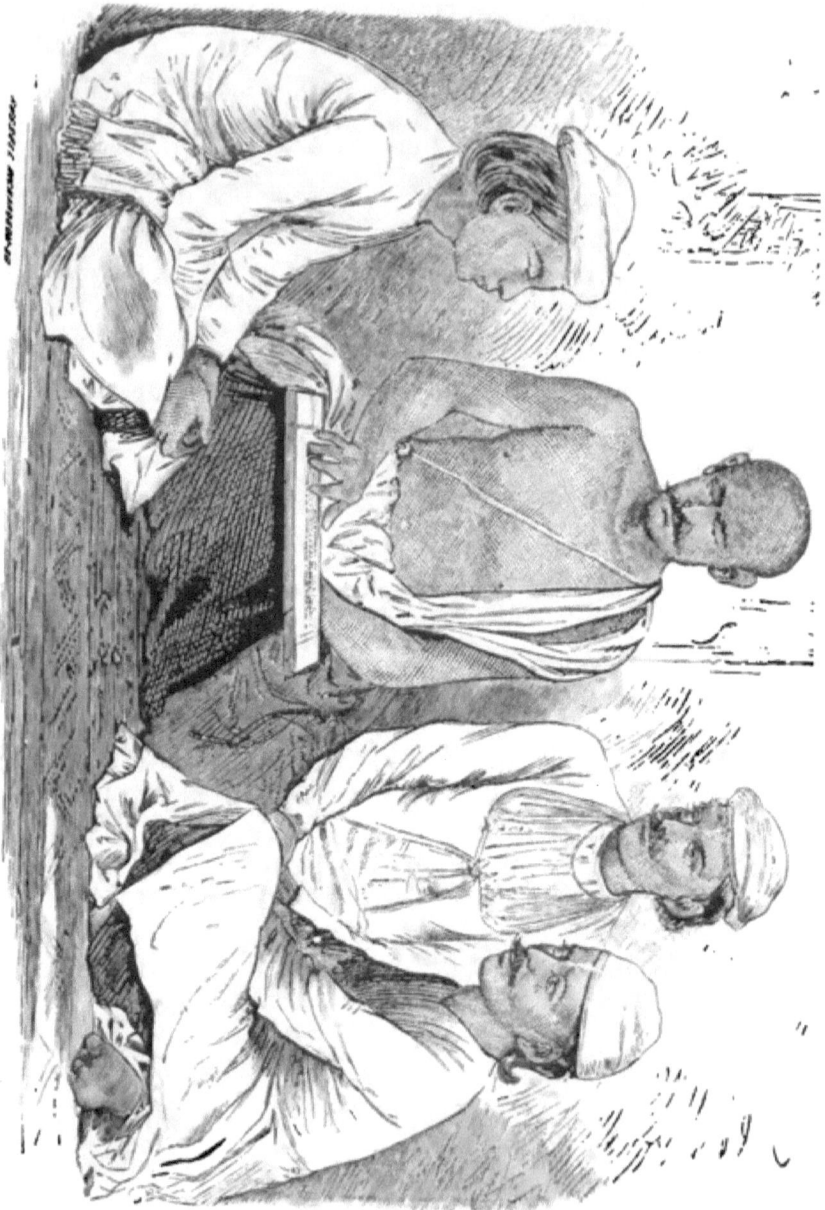

The Hindus and their Teacher.

pleasantly, "I am a missionary, old man, come to see you."

"Why have you come here?" demanded the fakir threateningly.

"Come to see you, my old friend," said the doctor.

"No one is permitted to come here," growled the devotee.

"You see I have come," replied the missionary, with such good humor that the old man's rigid features relaxed and his lips wore a smile.

Encouraged by his changed aspect, Dr. Scott asked him several questions concerning his faith and hope, to which he replied with the usual conceit of his class. Finally the missionary asked, "Have you a wife and children?" This question excited him to rage. "Don't use such language here!" said he. The doctor apologized, and thus restored the old man to partial good humor. Nevertheless, he requested Dr. Scott to leave, and, starting before him, led the way out. As the missionary followed, he asked, "What do you eat, old man?"

Putting on a mysterious manner the poor creature said, "God feeds me."

"Do you eat the fruit of these mango-trees?"

"Do the trees bear fruit twelve months?" he replied.

"But who feeds you?"

"God, I tell you."

This was said with increasing sharpness, and the doctor bade him adieu and passed out from his wretched retreat. As he was leaving the neighborhood a superstitious old man told him some wonderful stories of the fakir, such as that he lived without eating, and that he could work almost any miracle. "No," said the missionary, "you are a better man than he, for he seems to be very ill-tempered indeed." The old man bowed and felt flattered. The doctor walked away, musing in his heart over the conceit, self-deception, and misery of the old fakir hermit.

While Dr. Scott was talking one day to some village people a native said to a passer-by, "Come and hear of salvation!" This was uttered with a most sardonic leer. Dr. Scott entreated him not to trifle with so serious a matter, after which the fellow left the assembly saying, "Give me a village, and I will become a Christian."

In one village a Moslem teacher stirred up some fellows of the baser sort to ask Dr. Scott impertinent questions. The doctor ceased talking, when the Moslem pushed a coarse, brazen-faced fellow forward to make a pretended reply. Seeing that nothing good could be accomplished, Dr. Scott, after rebuking the Moslem, rose up and left. As he walked away the crowd followed him, hooting uproariously and clapping hands. To this gross insult Dr. Scott only suggested that, if he should report their conduct to the English authorities, they would all be punished. This intimation silenced them at once, and the Moslem teacher abjectly apologized for the uproar. The fellow did not fear God, but both he and the villagers stood in awe of British law.

In another village where the people heard Dr. Scott with attention, an objector asked a question which he evidently thought would confound the doctor. "If Christ be God," said he, "and a true incarnation, let him appear and show himself to us this evening, and we will believe on him."

"Do you think Ram a true incarnation?" responded Dr. Scott.

"Yes," rejoined the objector with emphasis.

"Well," retorted the missionary, "if Ram be a true incarnation, let him appear this evening, and I will believe on him." The objector, covered with confusion, made no reply.

When the English were digging a canal which was to be fed by deflecting the water of the Ganges from its natural course, the Brahmins declared that their sacred river would never consent to quit its ancient bed. Unfortunately for the prophetic reputation of the Brahmins, the river did flow into the canal. Then, to save their wounded influence, the idolaters spread a report that the river was only prevailed on to enter the canal by costly offerings from the British! This cunning lie Dr. Scott denounced one day, and was hissed and hooted in the most noisy and contemptuous manner. Facing the leaders of this uproar, he bade them remember their British rulers. This was enough. They became as "meek and submissive as lambs."

Dr. Scott asked a careless Zemindar one day, "What do you think becomes of the spirit at death?"

With an indifferent air he replied, "O, it goes out like this, [here he sent a whiff of air from his mouth,] and that is the end of it, I suppose." Evidently the poor creature was living without God and without hope.

At Baharepoor, amid a crowd of hearers, some base fellows asked Dr. Scott impertinent questions, ridiculed the doctrines he taught, laughed at his singing, impudently asking him to sing again. The doctor requested his native assistant to exhort, which he did, warning them of their danger of hell.

"O," they replied, "it would be no better for us if we became Christians. There is Moses Peters, [a renegade from the faith,] he is the greatest liar, rogue, and licentious man in the village."

In vain Dr. Scott assured them that Moses Peters was not recognized as a Christian. Their hostility was too strong to be overcome, and the doctor left.

One day an old man asked our missionary, "If we become Christians where shall we go for wives for our sons, or who will come for our daughters?"

Perceiving that this question was seriously, honestly put, the doctor pointed out that there were many Christian families growing up in India between which marriages could be formed; but the old man went away seemingly delighted to think that he had stumbled on an insurmountable obstacle to the Christian religion. His theory of *caste* had blinded his eyes.

"There is no sin in this village," cried a man in a village meeting at Mai Budea, as the missionary was speaking of the evil of sin and of its remedy. Instantly a half-score of voices responded in concert, "We have plenty of sin here!" The objector was thus silenced by his own countrymen, who, though willing to confess their sins, were not ready to be saved from them by Jesus Christ.

"The gods will surely destroy us in anger if we turn to Christ," said an objector to a missionary at Dawari.

"If they have power to harm any one," replied the man of God, "let them destroy us first."

This fear of the anger of their gods is a common plea among the Hindus; but, says Dr. Scott, "this silly fear will not last forever."

"The Ganga Jee (the Ganges) is a great goddess. We worship her because of her great benefits." Thus spoke a bigoted objector who, with a swelling air, walked into a group of Hindus to whom a missionary was talking on the banks of the Ganges.

"But," replied the missionary, "grass also is of great use to man. Why not worship it?"

"You try and live on grass four days, and you will see of what use it is for man," retorted the objector triumphantly.

"And you try Ganges water for four days, and see how useless it is for food," rejoined the missionary. If not convinced, the fellow was, at least, silenced.

"I worship the sun," said a shop-keeper to Dr. Scott, who had been showing some Hindus the folly of expecting to get rid of sin by washing in the waters of the Ganges. The doctor looked at the sun-worshiper and replied, "Then you, too, are a great idolater."

The man retorted, "But you English people also worship the sun, and have a day set apart for it."

"Not now," said the doctor. "We have learned the truth from Christ, and no longer worship the sun."

"Why not?" queried the shop-keeper.

"Suppose you hang a lamp in your shop to give light to purchasers, and some one should come along and, instead of saluting you, should salute your lamp, what would you think of him?"

The amused look of the listeners showed that they enjoyed the overthrow of the now silent sun-worshiper. But to see folly is not to abandon it.

"What benefit will we receive if we become Christians?" asked a Hindu one day.

The missionary replied by inquiring, "What kind of benefit do you want?"

"Food and clothing and lands," rejoined the man.

"But," said the missionary, "do you crave no other good?"

"What else do we need?" asked the objector. The missionary pointed out the needs of the soul, to which the objector replied that the Hindu's religion met those wants. The missionary then appealed to the wickedness of the Hindus, and was told that Europeans were wicked too. This charge led to an explanation of the difference between nominal and real Christians; but it was apparent that the vices of nominal Christians were both excuses and stumbling-blocks to the heathen Hindu. Shame on Christian men who, not being true to their name, are stumbling-blocks to heathens!

The peepul-tree is an object of worship in India. A native teacher, named Paul, said to a crowd one day, "You regard the peepul-tree as a god, and adore and worship it as a protector, but while you put the sacred thread around it, and are standing worshiping at one side, along comes a camel, which, stretching up its long neck, proceeds to make a meal from your god on the other. Your god cannot save himself from being devoured by an animal."

The crowd laughed heartily at this and similar illustrations of the folly of idolatry, and finally left, apparently well pleased at the merriment that had been made at the expense of their gods. Manifestly their devotion to idols cannot be either profound or sincere. Let us hope that, seeing its folly, they will soon be won to the worship of Him whose glory is above all created things!

A Brahmin visited Dr. Scott during a fair on the banks of the Ganges, and confessed that he had learned to doubt the truth of his religion, and that he was inclined to accept Christianity. He said he still conformed to the popular customs, but only to escape annoyance. He would not openly declare his Christian convictions, because, by so doing, he would lose his means of support. "In numerous instances," remarks the doctor, "genuine inquirers stumble at this difficulty." It is a real one, and will remain until the non-Christian population cease to combine for the purpose of depriving converts of their means of livelihood. Yet even now faith often proves stronger than fear, and many converts heroically profess Christ, even in face of threatening starvation.

While passing through the village of Kuar, Dr. Scott and his native helpers, on turning a corner, came upon a group of children. Instantly the little folks turned and ran off, exclaiming, "Run! Here they come who tell about Jesus!"

No doubt these little ones had been taught by their mothers to avoid Christian teachers, lest they should be carried to a foreign land, or be bewitched and changed into Christians against their will. Alas, poor children! Could they but hear Jesus say, "Suffer little children to come unto me," many of them would call upon him, as thousands have already learned to do.

"If it is in our fate, we will adopt your religion," was a frequent response of the people to Dr. Scott, when he urged them to be saved. The popular belief in India is, that inside the skull bone of the forehead all the acts and events of a man's life are unalterably traced by the pen of fate. Hence they ascribe every thing to *kismet*, or fate. Kismet is very much of a hinderance to the missionary in all Oriental lands.

Dr. Morrison's first Chinese teacher was Yong Sam Tak, a proud, dogmatic man. Morrison, then a young man, soon sought to talk with him about religion; but the typical heathen refused, and expressed his aversion to the truth by saying, "My country not custom to talky of God's business."

In Christian lands women are more easily won to the service of Christ than men. In India they are harder to be persuaded. An example of this fact is seen in Ajeet Sing, (unconquerable lion,) the chief man in the village of Lukempore. He heard Dr. Scott preach, and seemed likely to become a convert. But his two wives, with other village women, besought him, with tears and threats, not to become a Christian, and he yielded to their entreaties. Dr. Scott remarks, that, as a result of their greater ignorance and superstition, generally the women of India are the greatest enemies of the missionaries.

Another illustration of their hostility to our Christ was seen when Dr. Scott asked a Mohammedan farmer of wealth, "Why, if you are sincere, do you not seek baptism?" This man had been an inquirer at the mission house nearly two years. He replied, "Because my wife refuses to come with me, and, as you will not promise to secure me another wife, I cannot take that step." This answer was decisive. He preferred the approval of his wife to the favor of Christ, thus proving that he was unworthy of admission to the kingdom of God.

During one of his missionary tours in India, Dr. Scott was obliged to lodge in the mud hut of a native helper. A disgusting odor reminded him that the hovel must have been used to house goats. Smoke from the hearth filled his narrow room and tortured his eyes. A school of boys, actually yelling their lessons, was kept in an adjoining room. There was very little comfort to be taken in such a lodging; but the doctor remarks, "If God only blesses our entrance among this people with the salvation of souls, what a glorious reward!" While on his way to the Himalayas, in pursuit of health, Dr. Scott was overtaken by the darkness. He and his party missed their way. The road was rocky and dangerous. Wild beasts ranged the mountains. Shelter must be found somewhere. Presently they reached a portion of a turbulent stream which they thought was a ford. Dr. Scott drove his pony into the river. The creature soon lost its foothold. The water flowed over the saddle. The pony kept on, now swimming, now floundering, until it seemed that both horse and rider must perish. But both were plucky, and finally the pony, with his dripping rider, reached the opposite shore and scrambled up the steep bank. Dr. Scott soon found a planter's bungalow. Natives were sent out to bring in the rest of the party, and thus the peril was happily escaped.

THE END.

www.ingramcontent.com/pod-product-compliance
Lightning Source LLC
Chambersburg PA
CBHW032053230426
43672CB00009B/1582